Dear Sister,

Dear Sister,

Letters of Hope and Encouragement

Gisela Yohannan

BOOKS

a division of Gospel for Asia

www.gfa.org

ISBN: 978-1-59589-049-8

Published by gfa books, a division of Gospel for Asia
1800 Golden Trail Court, Carrollton, TX 75010
1-800-WIN-ASIA

Printed in the United States of America

For more information about other materials,
visit our website: www.gfa.org.

12 13 14 15 16 17 18 19 20 Y/I 10 9 8 7 6 5 4

Dedication

I dedicate this book to my loving daughter, Sarah, who is very special to me. After finishing her studies in the States, she chose to go to seminary in India and become a missionary. I miss her very much, but I am so thankful that she has decided to invest her life to help reach the unreached in Asia.

Table of Contents

Acknowledgments

This book represents my journey with the Lord for the past seven years and the lessons He taught me for my own life.

I have shared these lessons with thousands of women in letters, with the hope of strengthening them in their walk with Jesus. We have now compiled these letters in this book to make them available to other believers as well.

I am grateful to Heidi Chupp, Kim Smith and everyone else who had a part in producing this book. My special thanks goes to my dear husband, K.P. Yohannan, for reviewing the book and giving his valuable advice.

Introduction

For the past seven years I have been writing letters to the wives of our pastors and missionaries, as well as all the other sisters who are part of our ministry in many countries. It has been a joy and privilege for me to encourage each one in her personal walk with the Lord and in her ministry.

Because each letter deals with a specific subject relevant to following and serving Jesus, I decided to compile them in this book. That way not only our sisters, but also many others as well, can use them for their personal or group Bible studies.

I deliberately left the letters as they were originally written, including the introductions, dates and prayer requests, to preserve the time frame and personal style. With our ministry growing and changing continually, the events and statistics referred to in this book only correspond to the dates where they are mentioned in a particular letter.

My hope and prayer is that the lessons in this book will draw my sisters, and many of God's people, closer to Jesus and help them to live for Him.

Gisela Yohannan

1 Unity Validates Your Message

FEBRUARY 1999

Dear Sister,

Perhaps you are surprised to receive a letter from me. Actually, I would much rather visit you and get to know you personally. But even if I could travel twice as often as I do now, I still could not get to all the places where Gospel for Asia (GFA) works.

Did you know that GFA has more than 2,000 sisters in 11 countries, eastern and western, who are an important part of this ministry? Many of them are full-time workers on the mission field, in our training centers and offices. Others are wives of Believers Church pastors or GFA staff.

I strongly believe that the Lord wants to use every one of us sisters to touch the lives of millions of unreached people in Asia and help bring them to Jesus.

Since all of us are scattered across so many nations and mission fields, I asked our GFA leadership if I could start a bimonthly letter just to the sisters. They were happy to give their permission and set up a system so that you can receive my letters in your language.

The purpose of these letters is to encourage you in your calling and also help you realize that you are not alone, but are actually part of a large family that loves you and cares about you.

In each letter we will talk about one important issue that concerns us as sisters, so we can become better wives and servants of God. The letter will also include several specific prayer requests from our mission fields. This will give all of us the opportunity to pray together and believe God for definite answers. I am convinced that as we unite our hearts in intercession and in pursuing His purpose, God will draw us sisters together in unity, and we will begin to feel that indeed we are part of each others' lives and ministries.

In this first letter, I would like to share a few thoughts about why unity among us is extremely important to God. Please take the time to carefully read each Scripture reference you see.

We are to reflect God's nature. More than anything else, unity based on love, as described in 1 Corinthians 13:4–8, demonstrates the nature of God to a world that is torn into thousands of pieces by strife, wars and hatred. All these directly result from men's selfishness and pride, their demanding and fighting for their own rights at the expense of others.

God, on the other hand, is a Trinity that exists in perfect unity. God the Father, Jesus and the Holy Spirit never compete with each other for anything.

God's plan is that when people watch our lives, they should see a true reflection of His nature in us. That's why Jesus prayed for His followers just before He went to the cross: *"... that they may all be one; even as Thou, Father, art in Me, and I in Thee, that they also may be in Us"* (John 17:21).

Unity validates our Gospel message. Jesus clearly expresses in the very next statement of His prayer that the believability of the Gospel message will depend on our unity among each other: *"... that the world may believe that Thou didst send Me"* (John 17:21). It's a very serious and sobering truth. We generally think that preaching confirmed by healings and miracles will cause people to believe in Jesus. But now we discover in Jesus' prayer that unless God's work is backed up by our unity, we actually destroy the credibility of the Gospel. That should alarm us enough to honestly examine our home life, our teamwork and our relationships with our husband, co-workers, leaders and church members.

Unity transforms us into a mighty force. Imagine a cart with a heavy load on it and 20 people each trying to pull it into a different direction. How successful will they be to get to the next village? You know the answer. They will never make it unless they make up their minds and everyone pulls in the same direction.

Similarly, if people unite together in a cause, nothing will be impossible for them. That's what God said in Genesis 11:6 about the ungodly people who set out to build the Tower of Babel. How much truer should this statement be of us, whom God has called to build His kingdom!

Much frustration and lack of success in our ministries can often be traced back to the fact that our hearts are not united. If there is any resentment in your heart toward your leader, your co-worker, your husband or the ministry—even if you never express it in words—you have created a roadblock for God's Spirit to move.

What all could happen? Imagine for a moment—what could happen in your home, your mission field, our GFA ministry and your nation:

> ... if you and your husband were truly united in reaching the lost, and you would no longer seek for a comfortable life?

> ... if you and your co-workers would stop envying each other's gifts and there would be unity on the team?

> ... if we as 2,000 sisters began to pray daily for one another and the lost world, and God could mold us together into a powerful force whose only desire was to reach Asia for Christ?

Unity does not come without a price! It starts with a deliberate decision on our part to humble ourselves as Jesus did, to willingly lay down our rights and desires and submit to the will of God with all our heart (Philippians 2:5–8).

If we struggle to hold on to something we count so dear, let us consider this: Our life here on earth is so short. Unless we make our decisions with eternity in mind, we will definitely miss God's plan.

My dear Sister, may I suggest that you save this letter so you can study this issue of unity further, whether privately, with your co-workers or during your regular GFA sisters' meeting. The most important thing is to ask yourself after each point, "How can I practically apply what God has shown me?" Unless you make specific decisions and take actual steps to implement them, you will not experience any spiritual growth in this area of unity. My sincere prayer is that all of us sisters will desire to become one in Jesus and be used by Him.

I invite you now to pray with us and believe God to meet the following needs:

- Between now and the end of March, 2,500 students will graduate from our 31 Bible schools in India, Nepal, Myanmar, Sri Lanka, Sikkim and Bhutan. Pray for God's anointing and protection for these young brothers and sisters as they are sent out as missionaries to many unreached villages.

- Pray for all of our GFA sisters, that God would unite our hearts and we will truly begin to live for this one purpose: to reach the unreached of our nations with the Gospel of Jesus Christ.

I love you in Jesus and look forward to meeting you some day.

Your sister,

Gisela

2 Teaching by Example

APRIL 1999

Dear Sister,

I just returned home from a visit to Myanmar. Along with Brother Ebenezer, our missions director for Southeast Asia, I had the privilege of attending the graduation of our Gospel for Asia training center in Yangon. It was so exciting to watch 53 young men and women receive their diplomas. When I looked at their faces, I saw such joy and sincerity that my heart was filled with great hope. I felt these young people were 53 grains of wheat in the hands of Jesus, willing to be placed into the soil of Myanmar to die and bring forth much fruit.

Brother Chum, GFA's leader for Myanmar, and his co-workers are so grateful for what God has done. The school started in 1992 with a few students in a small rented place and an office under a tree. Today, more than 250 students are studying at our GFA training center in Yangon, which has become the second-largest Bible school in Myanmar.

Because I had to catch my flights to Myanmar from Delhi, India, I had the chance to spend some time with our son, Daniel, who is currently serving the Lord in North India. It was a real blessing for me to observe how the Lord is working in his life. My travel home took 10 hours longer than normal because of delays and two missed connections.

In this letter, I would like to share a few thoughts with you that I have found to be very important in serving the Lord.

Did you know that even if you never presented one lesson in a Sunday school class, God specifically chose you to be a teacher? You see, there is another way of teaching besides lecturing. It's the one Paul describes in 1 Timothy 4:12 and Titus 2:7: *"... be an example."*

The most powerful teaching is not with words, but by example. Our lives are designated by God to become models for others to observe and learn how biblical truth is translated into everyday life.

Jesus revolutionized our understanding of God by what He did *after* His sermons: touching lepers, taking time to embrace and bless children, walking away when people tried to make Him king, washing the disciples' feet and praying for those who crucified Him.

Likewise, Paul trained his co-workers and converts by his example: going back to the place where he was stoned to preach again, singing praises to God at midnight after being beaten and jailed and fervently praying for the churches and writing letters to them—while waiting for his execution in a Roman prison.

The strongest influence on our own children, our Bible school students and the believers in our churches is our example. It speaks much louder than words.

Our example reproduces in others what we are ourselves. The pattern they see in us, good or bad, becomes their teacher. If we put God first, they will too. If our walk with the Lord is consistent, our faith unshakable, our lives free of bitterness and our hearts full of forgiveness, that's what those around us will become as well.

But believe me, our negative attitudes, our insincerity, our carelessness and our secret greediness for money and material things will transfer just as strongly. And it bears enormous consequences for God's kingdom. Those who are taught by your example will pass the same on to others. Take a good look at the things you don't like in your children, co-workers, Bible school students or church members and ask yourself: "What did *I* contribute to create this?"

We are automatically teachers as long as just one person observes us! My dear Sister, that's the thing we most often forget. For those of us who are married, it is easy to complain in the privacy of our heart or in front of our children that the ministry is robbing us of the good things in life. Even if we never put it in words, the atmosphere we create is incredibly destructive and teaches volumes to those watching us.

That's one of the main reasons why many children of Gospel workers resent their parents' ministry and choose a secular job rather than serving the Lord.

When our children were born, I decided that I would not allow any resentful attitude to take root in my heart and that I would never talk negatively about serving the Lord in front of

Daniel and Sarah. Yes, there were times that I cried when my husband had to travel so much and we three were often alone. But I always told our children, "Jesus is worth it, and we are privileged to help others come to know Him." I made sure that they knew I was in total agreement with what my husband was doing.

"Follow my example" was Paul's invitation to the Christians. Please read 1 Corinthians 11:1, Philippians 3:17 and 4:9, and 1 Thessalonians 1:6–7 and 2:8. Paul didn't write this because he felt he was perfect, but because he knew he was genuine in his faith and pursuit of Christ.

I believe the Lord desires that each of us come to a place where He can point to our life for others to learn what it truly means to follow Jesus. Perhaps by reading this letter, you have discovered an area in your life where your example created un-Christlike attitudes in others. Bring this area to the Lord in prayer and, by His grace, change the direction you were going. Be humble, and confess to your children or co-workers that your influence taught them the wrong thing. Most of all, let them see how Jesus has changed your heart.

Please join us in prayer for our Myanmar mission field:

- Pray for the 53 graduates as they make decisions for their future ministries.

- Our present training center dormitories are made of bamboo. Pray for a building permit to construct a permanent building.

- Pray for Brother Chum and for all our GFA leadership and missionaries as they share the love of Jesus in this closed country.

Dear Sister, I sincerely hope this letter is an encouragement for your walk with the Lord. May God bless you and fill your heart with His peace.

Your sister,

Gisela

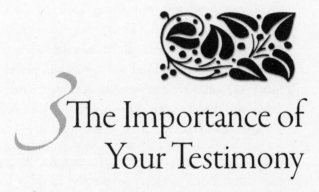

3 The Importance of Your Testimony

JUNE 1999

Dear Sister,

Since I wrote you last, I traveled to Kerala, India, to attend the graduation of our daughter Sarah from the Gospel for Asia Biblical Seminary (ABS). My husband and our son were there as well, and we enjoyed being together as a family for two weeks. Daniel has now returned to North India, and Sarah decided to come home for a month before she goes back to India for ministry.

It's such fun to have Sarah at home, and I know I will miss her even more when she leaves in a few weeks. But I am so very grateful that both of our children desire to serve the Lord, and I am determined not to hold them back. Instead, I want to encourage them to give their all for Jesus.

When I look at them now, I am often reminded of what I wrote by faith so many years ago in my book *Mate and Helpmate:*

> I am sure as Daniel and Sarah grow up I will miss them not being small any more. But there is a day coming in their lives I am looking forward to—by faith. Before our children were born, we dedicated both of them to the Lord and we asked Him to save them and to call them for mission work. It will truly be the most wonderful day of my life when the Lord will answer this prayer.... I believe I will not fear to lose them as they become adults, but my joy will be even greater, knowing the Lord will call them and use their lives to bring glory to His name.

Because of the very nature of my husband's calling, our family is quite visible, both to God's people and to those who oppose Christianity as well. I know the same is true for you in the place where the Lord has asked you to serve Him. That's why I want to share a few thoughts with you on the importance of your testimony.

Our lives are made visible to others by God's choice. If you are like me, you prefer to be more private and selective of what others should know about you and your family life.

But God has other ideas. He is trying to save a world that does not know Him or His Word. That's why He chose to provide them with a living example of His grace—you. His intention is this: As they observe you, they can clearly see how God could transform their lives if they trusted Him. In addition, God is building a church with people who often come straight from heathen backgrounds. These new believers need to have the opportunity to watch and learn from someone living the Christian life before their eyes.

Paul is writing about all this in 2 Corinthians 3:2–3: *"You are our letter . . . known and read by all men. . . . You are a letter of Christ. . . ."*

It's not easy to be observed 24 hours a day. It puts enormous responsibility on us to live worthy of our calling and to be that example for others to follow.

As adults, we find it difficult to be watched so closely, but our children feel the pressure even more. Church members usually have much higher expectations of the pastor's children than they have of their own. Consequently, the pastor's children often receive more criticism from people, a longer list of do's and don'ts from their parents and more punishment for their shortcomings. All this can easily result in discouragement, resentment toward God and the wish to have nothing to do with ministry.

But by far the greatest danger is for your child to become a hypocrite, which can easily occur if he is constantly told to behave in a certain way, "otherwise, what might people think?" This teaches him to act out a spirituality before people that he does not have. Eventually, he will be more concerned about pleasing people than pleasing God.

God never intended our testimony to be an extra strain. It should be the natural outcome of our normal, everyday walk with Him. He never meant for us to give an extra performance before the world! All He wanted was to let them see how Jesus lives through us.

If there is no difference between how I act at home or in church or how I talk to my husband and children in private or public, my testimony will have great power. In addition, my children will see a reality in my life that will protect them from becoming actors instead of disciples.

God doesn't expect perfect performance. He looks for faithfulness and sincerity in the testimony we have for Him before the world. When He decided to display our life to those around us, He knew well how weak and fragile we are. How is it, then, that He still wants others to watch our lives?

God wants to demonstrate how His grace and power are sufficient in our weakness. He also wants for the world to see how true Christians humble themselves, confess their sins, love one another, ask for forgiveness, love their enemies, persevere under trials, exercise faith, trust the Lord in difficult circumstances and are faithful until death.

The devil will do all he can to destroy your testimony. Don't be fooled even for a minute to think the devil has no interest in you because you are "just" the pastor's wife or an ordinary member of your Gospel team. You are a target for the enemy, because whatever you do will deeply affect the credibility of your husband's ministry or the effectiveness of your Gospel team. In fact, the more your life and ministry are visible, the greater interest the devil has in causing you or another member of your family to stumble, at the same time discrediting the name of the Lord and discouraging other believers.

Temptations, false accusations, sickness, discouragement, the lure of materialism, opportunities to compromise the truth, lies, the cares of this world, disappointment, misunderstandings between you and your husband or co-workers—these are just a few of the things the devil will use to trip you up.

God is well able to keep us. Knowing about the devil's intentions should not fill us with fear, but instead keep us on the alert. *"Greater is He who is in you than he who is in the world"* (1 John 4:4) is God's promise to us. To give the devil no opportunity to destroy your testimony, do these things:

- Walk in humility before God, knowing that you need His grace every moment of your life.

- Flee temptation and anything that could cause you to compromise.

- Never allow sin, bitterness and resentment to put down roots in your heart.

- Forgive others.

- Pray daily for yourself, your husband, your children and your co-workers, that you will all stay faithful to Jesus.

Please pray and trust the Lord together with us for these things:

- Pray for the thousands of GFA Bible school students whose classes are starting this month. For many of them, it's their first time away from home.

- Pray for our teachers, that God will give them wisdom to teach and grace to be a living instruction.

I consider it a special privilege to write to you and be a small part of your life.

Your sister,

Gisela

4 Do You Have Room in Your Heart for Others?

August 1999

Dear Sister,

I was very excited and curious when our Indian office translated and forwarded a number of letters that some of the sisters wrote to me. It was nice to read their encouraging words and learn a little about their lives. I thought that perhaps I should also tell you a little about the things I am doing.

Besides being a housewife, I am working with our GFA Publications Department. Some of my responsibilities include writing letters, reports from the mission field and articles for several of our publications. These help our prayer partners understand what God is doing and know how to intercede for the needs on the field. Several times a year, I travel to different GFA training centers or visit some of our mission fields. During these trips, I share with our students or hold ladies' meetings to encourage our GFA sisters. Basically, I want to be willing to do whatever the Lord asks of me to help my husband fulfill the calling God has placed on his life.

In this letter I would like to share with you a few thoughts about self-centeredness.

I believe the Lord desires that we make room in our hearts for each other. Most people's lives only revolve around themselves, their families and their possessions. Perhaps we grew up with strong family ties, and we were taught that all our efforts, energy and resources should benefit our own family. But when we look in the Bible, we discover that as believers, God has called us to far more:

> *But with humility of mind let each of you regard one another as more important than himself; do not merely look out for your own personal interests, but also for the interests of others* (Philippians 2:3–4).

God expects my focus to change from me to you. This Scripture actually means that your spiritual and physical well-being must become my deep personal concern. I will no longer be satisfied if my own life exhibits love, joy, peace, humility and holiness; but I will earnestly desire for God to develop these things in you as well. I will not rest but will seek the Lord on your behalf until my prayers are answered. In fact, my concern for you will run so deeply that I will only consider my victory in the race complete if you cross the finish line alongside of me.

Your suffering, poverty, struggles or failures will cause me to feel the same pain and sadness you experience, and I will look for ways to help you. On the other hand, if you do well and God uses you, I will not be jealous but will rejoice and praise God for you.

Why do we have so little genuine interest in each other? Because we are so hopelessly selfish. Even in our seemingly selfless service as wives and mothers, we are self-centered. We do all these wonderful things for our husband, expecting his devotion, love and care for us in response. Our children get our greatest attention and sacrificial love, but at the same time we expect that their lives will benefit us in the future.

We regard our headache, our disappointments or our lack of finances as the most important event in the universe. Sadly, our curiosity, jealousy and gossip or the benefits we get from our relationships very often motivate our so-called interest in each other. But none of these things even faintly resembles what God had in mind. Even in the ministry, we expect things to revolve around us; otherwise, our happiness is gone. The truth is, we have no real interest in each other, because we are so filled up with our own selves. There is no room, time or energy left for anyone else.

What does it take for us to change?

Dying to ourselves. The apostle Paul wrote in Galatians 2:20: *"I have been crucified with Christ; and it is no longer I who live, but Christ lives in me."*

Because we are "dead," we will offer no resistance for Christ to freely live through us. From now on, His love can flow unhindered through us toward others. But even though this is absolutely true, we so often cling to our old, unsaved ways and block everything Christ wants to do by our self-centeredness.

So how can that death, which I died with Christ on the cross, overtake those still unsurrendered areas in my life? It starts with denying myself and picking up my cross *daily* in order to follow in the footsteps of Jesus (see Luke 9:23). This means every morning when I get up, I must make a fresh decision to deliberately say "no" to my rights, my desires and myself—and say "yes" to the will of God.

Falling in love with Jesus. In the measure in which our love for the person of Jesus (not the benefits we get from Him) increases, our self-love will decrease and make room for our brothers and sisters:

> *Beloved, let us love one another, for love is from God; and every one who loves is born of God and knows God. The one who does not love does not know God, for God is love* (1 John 4:7–8).

Understanding what it truly means to be a member of the Body of Christ. *"So we, who are many, are one body in Christ, and individually members one of another"* (Romans 12:5).

Many times, with our words or actions, we carelessly or deliberately inflict wounds on our brothers and sisters. In some cases, we even amputate them from the rest of the Body of Christ. I believe it happens mostly because we don't see ourselves as one living, breathing organism in which each part is extremely essential in order for the whole body to function and to survive. If we understood this, we would care for each other just like we read in Philippians 2:3–4.

My dear Sister, God knows that each of us has much to learn in this area of making room in our hearts for each other. But today let us make a decision to change by the grace of God.

Now I would like to invite you to join us in prayer and faith for the following needs:

- Pray for the upcoming elections in India, that the Lord will preserve our freedom to preach the Gospel.

- Malaria is spreading rapidly through the region around our training center in Assam, India. One of our students and a Believers Church worker recently died. Please pray for their families and for God's protection for all our students and workers.

May the Lord comfort and bless you today with His nearness.

Your sister,

Gisela

5 Transformation Starts with Your Mind

OCTOBER 1999

Dear Sister,

I am sitting in my kitchen writing this letter to you. As I do, I try to imagine where you might be and what you are doing today. I often think about the sisters I have met in some of our GFA training centers or on the mission field, and I wonder what has become of them.

Last week in a GFA report I read about one of our Believers Churches in Himachal Pradesh, India. When I saw the name of the pastor, I became very excited because two years ago I met his wife, Nirmala, in our ladies' training center in Haryana, India. Nirmala had left her two small children with her husband and father-in-law so she could receive training to do women's ministry in this needy state. Her commitment and burden for the lost have challenged all those who heard her story.

Perhaps the next time, when I read field reports, your name will come up!

Today I would like to write to you about something that determines our usefulness to God on this earth.

It is astonishing to read, in Romans 8:29, the high goal that God has for our life: "*. . . to become conformed to the image of His Son.*" This, declares the apostle Paul, is an ongoing transformation: "*But we all . . . are being transformed into the same image from glory to glory*" (2 Corinthians 3:18). Though this transformation will not be complete until we reach heaven, we are definitely expected to grow closer to the likeness of Jesus with every passing day. Our obedience, submission, love, service and our entire character should increasingly resemble His.

But why then have many believers made little or no progress at all since they were saved? Why is their love for the world still greater than their love for God? Why, even after 5 or 10 years, do they remain full of unforgiveness, greed, strife, selfishness and jealousy? And if corrected, why do they still fight back or justify their wrong attitudes?

What happened to the transformation that was supposed to take place? Most often, the transformation is hindered or greatly delayed because these Christians, though they are new creations in Christ, have retained their old, corrupt mind-set. That old mind-set gives them the wrong signals and causes them to act in an un-Christlike manner. You see, our mind-set will always determine our attitudes, words and actions.

The Bible tells us very clearly how this transformation into the image of Christ must happen: *"And do not be conformed to this world, but be transformed by the renewing of your mind"* (Romans 12:2). Unless it starts with renewing our mind, this transformation into the image of Christ will not work. No matter how hard we may try, sooner or later we will revert back to our old ways. Our goal must be to renew our mind first, because everything else we do is based on our mind-set.

Paul tells us how this renewed mind should look when he exhorts us in Philippians 2:5, *"Let this mind be in you which was also in Christ Jesus"* (NKJV). In the following verses, he explains that Christ's mind-set was the starting point of His willingness to empty Himself of His divine privileges, take human form and become obedient until His death on the cross.

Just imagine for a moment that your mind was renewed to the point where you took on Christ's attitudes. No doubt it would significantly change the way you respond to others. Moreover, it would no longer be a strenuous, artificial effort to love others, serve them, forgive and submit yourself to authority. It would naturally flow out of your life, because your new mind-set would cause you to act in accordance with the nature of Christ.

But how can we renew our mind?

1. Cooperate with God. Decide to work *with* God, not against Him, as He begins to change you. Never be satisfied with what you are right now or try to excuse your un-Christlike attitudes and actions. Tell the Lord from the depths of your heart, "Lord, I want to become what You say I can become. I am willing to accept whatever it takes for You to bring me there."

2. Accept correction and rebuke with humility. From whatever source the correction or rebuke might come, receive it as from the Lord. See God's love for you in it, and be thankful that He cares enough to point out the things you must change.

3. Fill your whole being with the Word of God. Through the Word of God we know His nature, will, love, plans, thoughts, actions, power, salvation, principles, promises and everything we need to live for Him. If we want our mind renewed, this is the source we *must* use. Please read Colossians 3:16, Joshua 1:8, Hebrews 4:12 and John 8:31–32.

Read, study and meditate on God's Word at every opportunity. Throughout the day, when you clean your house, cook or wash dishes, let your mind dwell on Scripture instead of problems or gossip. Desire above everything else to learn and understand God's Word. Ask the Holy Spirit to teach you.

Live what you learn, and don't make compromises because of your culture or traditions. Whenever you encounter something contrary to what you live, immediately accept what the Scripture says as your new direction.

4. Watch carefully what you permit your mind to dwell on. Don't entertain thoughts that you know are contrary to the mind of Christ. It will seriously hinder your mind from being renewed and with it, the transformation of your life into the image of Christ.

I hope these thoughts will encourage you to desire to become all that God has planned for you.

Please pray with us for our GFA women's ministry:

• Pray for our new ladies' training center in Kerala, India. It started in August with 55 sisters.

• Pray for the effectiveness and protection of our girls' teams that are doing outreach ministry. Several of these teams have reported threats and serious harassment.

May you daily be aware of the grace of God and His love for you.

Your sister in Christ,

Gisela

6 Whose Vision Is It to Reach the Unreached?

Dear Sister,

This month of December is very special to me. By the time you get this letter, I will be traveling home from visiting different mission fields in India. My husband and our children, Daniel and Sarah, will join me a week later; and for the first time in five years, we will celebrate Christmas at home. I am looking forward to this very much, and I thank God for making it possible for us to be together as a family.

We can most clearly see the love of God for a lost humanity by this: God sent His only Son, Jesus, into this world as a baby, so that He could die on the cross for our redemption 33 years later. This Christmas, remembering the birth of our Savior should fill our hearts with great joy, deep gratitude and a burden and vision to reach the lost.

In this letter I would like to draw your attention to the vision and purpose God has given all of us here at Gospel for Asia.

Reaching the most unreached in our generation—This is the one thing we believe God has called us to live for and invest our lives in. My dear Sister, since you are part of this ministry, have you taken time to think about this statement? Have you asked God for your specific place in this vision? Perhaps you already know your place. But have you really taken it? Have you made GFA's vision your vision?

In our GFA ministry, there are many sisters who have a deep burden for the lost and daily lay down their lives to reach them. But we also have others who struggle in this area.

At every pastors' conference there are some brothers who are deeply discouraged and don't know what to do next, because their wives don't share their vision for the ministry God has entrusted to them.

Often when these brothers come home they find their wives in tears, weeping over the length of time they spent for the ministry, the lack of material things in their homes or the hardships of living on a pioneer field. Some of these sisters even stay home from church, refuse to go for any visitation and complain about their husbands to their neighbors and church members. These actions seriously hinder the ministry.

These dear sisters are deeply hurting because their expectations are not met. God knows their struggles and loves them just as much as those who don't have these conflicts. However, only two things will solve their problem: Either their husbands must give up the ministry and fulfill all their wives' expectations, or these sisters must join their husbands 100 percent in the vision God has given them. Anything less will not work!

The only biblical solution, however, is for the wife to join her husband in his vision. God clearly placed the husband as leader of the family, expecting his wife to accept and support his leadership. According to Genesis 2:18, she was created to be a helpmate for every area of his life and calling. And she will only find her greatest fulfillment and joy in God's purpose for her.

It may sound unfair that only the pastor's wife must lay down all her expectations and adopt her husband's missionary vision. What about him? Doesn't he have to give up something too? If he has answered God's call for full-time ministry, he has *already* given up his own plans for his life! The ministry he is doing now was God's idea, not his. So actually, equal sacrifice, obedience and commitment are required from both of them.

You see, whether we are single or married in full-time ministry or not, as believers in Christ we are not our own—we are bought with a price (1 Corinthians 6:19–20). We have no legal right to our lives. If we truly understood this truth, we would have less trouble surrendering our will.

Ultimately, it is really God's vision we refuse to accept. The vision to reach the unreached didn't originate with GFA, your husband or your team leader. It has been God's vision all along, ever since the fall of Adam. Please read Genesis 22:18, Matthew 28:19, John 3:16 and 2 Peter 3:9. As children of God, we are to reflect His image, and that includes His love and vision for the lost.

How is it possible for us to get this vision for the unreached if we don't have it?

1. Ask the Lord to give it to you. Jesus promised: *"If you ask Me anything in My name, I will do it"* (John 14:14).

2. Open your eyes and see the lives—and death—of those without Christ. Look at their suffering, hopelessness, bondage, fear and demonic oppressions. See them calling out in vain to their idol gods. Watch them die without peace and forgiveness of sin. And then say to yourself: "This would be me if I had never heard the Gospel."

3. Read what the Bible says about hell, and believe it. Then when you walk down the street and you see multitudes of people, tell yourself that hell is the eternal destination for each one of them, unless they have a chance to call upon the name of Jesus.

4. Cry out to the Lord to break your heart. Without love, compassion and tears, you will never have the vision to reach them.

5. Begin to pray for the lost in your village by name and ask the Lord to give you a chance to share the Gospel with them. You will be surprised at the opportunities God gives you, and your burden and vision will increase as you tell them about Jesus.

I now invite you to join us in prayer for these needs:

- Let's pray with compassion for all our sisters who struggle in this area we just discussed.

- Our training centers in Bangladesh and West Bengal, India, urgently need their own buildings.

This Christmas, may the love of God fill your heart and may you experience His peace.

I love you in Jesus,

Gisela

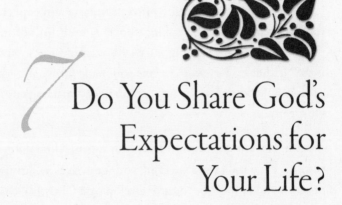

7 Do You Share God's Expectations for Your Life?

FEBRUARY 2000

Dear Sister,

For our family the new year started with a time of fellowship and prayer—and a phone call from my sister at 2 A.M. to let me know that my mother was seriously ill. Within a few hours, our daughter, Sarah, and I packed our suitcases and traveled to Germany to be with my mother.

As I write this letter, it's two weeks later, and by God's grace, my mother is doing much better.

Actually, for the first day of the new year my plans had been quite different. I was going to cook a nice dinner for our family.

Then I planned to take a few hours off to reflect on the past year, pray and think about what I should specifically believe God for during these next 12 months. I wanted to write those things down and make them a matter of prayer, faith and expectation.

This brings me to the question I wish to ask you:

Do you have any specific prayer requests and expectations for this year? I am not talking about a "wish list" of material things or ambitions you might have for your life, family and ministry. Neither do I mean the plans you made for your work, such as visiting 500 houses on your mission field or passing out 10,000 Gospel tracts.

What I want you to consider is your spiritual life: the depth of your personal walk with the Lord, your growth as a Christian, the progress you have made toward developing a Christlike character and, most of all, how real your relationship is with Jesus—if the things you proclaim can be seen in your life.

Our time here on earth is so limited, and the years we have to serve our God are so few, that it would be tragic if we let them pass by carelessly and simply live each day without being conscious of our purpose.

It takes God many years to train us and make us useful. The quality and depth of work we will be able to accomplish largely depends on the quality and depth God is able to work into our personal life and character. Our steadfastness, genuine love and trust in God's Word—and conversely, our shallowness, lack of faith and worldly mind-set—will all be reproduced in our disciples. May God give us grace to realize the seriousness of submitting to His hand when He works on our heart.

Why should we have expectations for our life as a child of God? Because God does! I believe that when He looks at each one of us, He sees not only our potential through Christ but also the finished result, and He longs to bring us there.

When Pharaoh's daughter opened the basket she found in the river, she saw a little Hebrew baby crying. But when God looked into that same basket He saw Moses, the deliverer of Israel.

When the inhabitants of Bethlehem watched David taking care of his father's sheep, they only saw a shepherd boy. But when God looked at him in the field tending his flock, He saw a king.

When people watched Peter following Jesus, they saw an uneducated fisherman. But Jesus saw a mighty apostle, filled with the Holy Spirit, leading His Church.

The highest expectation that God has for each of us surpasses that of a deliverer, a king or an apostle. He wants us to become like Jesus (Ephesians 4:13).

We need to agree with God and, with *all humility,* share His expectations for our lives. So often we have little or no expectations at all because we cannot see beyond our own small world and circumstances. Perhaps you also see yourself this way: poor, without opportunities in life, insignificant in the church, always struggling with problems, busy raising children, doing housework and having little time for spiritual pursuits.

But even if all these things were true, they are no hindrance for God to fulfill all He has in mind for your life. But He needs two things from your side: your cooperation and your faith! Remember, when Jesus touched the blind men's eyes, He said, *"Be it done to you according to your faith"* (Matthew 9:29).

At least once each year, we should take a serious look at our spiritual life, keeping God's expectations in mind. How do we know if we came a little closer to God's goal during the past 12 months? Look for signs like these:

- My tongue has become more hesitant to speak out, spread rumors and judge others.

- I find myself more often praying and doing something about the needs of others than my own.

- My conscience seems to speak louder and alert me faster to confess sin, forgive others and stay away from things that I would not have recognized as dangers to my spiritual life six months ago.

- Instead of depending on my team leader, co-workers or husband to rescue and comfort me each time in my struggles, I have become increasingly able to draw strength from the Lord on my own.

Evaluations like these don't make us more spiritual, but I have found that they are very helpful in determining what I should pray and believe for, search out in God's Word, work on and pursue for victory. Since it is still the beginning of the year, I suggest that you take a little time off and learn where you are in your walk with the Lord. Think of several areas where you struggle the most, and make them your specific prayer requests for this year. Expect that God will change you, and it will happen according to your faith.

Now I would like to invite you to earnestly pray for the Orissa, India, project which starts this month:

- For GFA's reconstruction of 200 houses in three Orissa villages wiped out by last year's cyclone.

- For safety of the workers and for the villagers to come to know the love of Jesus.

Remember, the Lord is well able to accomplish all He has set out to do in our lives.

Your sister,

Gisela

8 Only Believe!

APRIL 2000

Dear Sister,

This past February, Karen, one of our USA staff ladies, gave birth to a baby—10 weeks early. The little girl was healthy, but she weighed only 2 pounds, 14 ounces and had to receive special care in the hospital.

Imagine how difficult it must have been for Karen and her husband, Rod, to cling to the Lord's promises without being consumed by worry and fear. Praise God—the baby girl is doing very well; and by the time you get this letter, she will be at home with her parents and her brother, Brody.

All of us encounter situations where it is much easier to worry than to believe for a miracle. That's why I want to share a few thoughts with you from the story of Jairus in Mark 5.

The Answer is on its way. Jairus was so relieved when Jesus agreed to come to his house and heal his little daughter. He believed that if she could just hold on for a little while longer, she would be made well because Jesus, the Answer, was on His way.

But before they arrived at Jairus's home, news reached them that the child had died. The messengers advised the father not to trouble Jesus any longer, because it was too late.

At this point Jesus broke into the conversation with one goal in mind: to rescue Jairus's faith, which was about to be swallowed up by fear. Jesus said, *"Do not be afraid any longer, only believe"* (Mark 5:36). That doesn't seem like much to hold onto. But Jesus knew that as long as Jairus had faith, God could do the impossible for him—even in the face of death.

Why does God seek to reduce us to *"only believe"*?

1. Because usually when we face problems, we react just like Jairus:

> We believe . . . and we are anxious—all at the same time.

> We believe . . . and we worry.

> We believe . . . and we fear.

> We believe . . . and we weep and mourn.

> We believe . . . and we listen to the negative advice of our friends.

> We believe . . . and imagine the worst will happen.

2. God always looks for *pure faith,* not faith-plus-worry or faith-plus-fear, to be able to respond to our prayers. Jesus often

told those who received healing, *"Your faith has made you well"* (Mark 5:34; Luke 17:19). Not once did He say: "Your worry has made you whole." These words are recorded in the New Testament for our instruction, so that we may learn what it takes to receive from God.

3. "Only believe" protects our faith from getting killed. Jesus said to the father who begged Him to free his son from a demon: *"All things are possible to him who believes"* (Mark 9:23). And He told Martha, whose brother Lazarus had already been in the grave four days, *". . . if you believe, you will see the glory of God"* (John 11:40). Notice that Jesus only asked them to believe. You see, unless we leave everything else behind, our faith gets destroyed before we ever see the answer to our prayers.

Faith is an end product, or fruit, that develops from the Word of God we receive in our hearts. The Word of God is sown into our hearts like small seeds. As these seeds sprout, grow and mature, they will bear much fruit (Luke 8:11, 15). According to Romans 10:17, one of these fruits is faith: *"Faith comes from hearing, and hearing by the word of Christ."*

Watch over your faith. Our faith-fruit often gets destroyed before it ever reaches maturity. This happens when the Word of God encounters another type of plant in our heart that we have permitted to take root: thorns. *"And the seed which fell among the thorns, these are the ones who have heard, and as they go on their way they are choked with worries and riches and pleasures of this life, and bring no fruit to maturity"* (Luke 8:14).

There was nothing wrong with the ground into which the Word of God was sown. It wasn't hard or rocky. However, it wasn't weeded. The number-one thorn Jesus listed here was worry, which is the very thing we most frequently do when God asks us to *only believe.* And worry usually turns into fear and unbelief before we know it.

Watch the sparrows and consider the lilies—see how God takes care of them, and simply believe. That's what Jesus told His disciples when He listed some of their major worries in Luke 12:4–32 such as food, clothing, what they should say and the possibility of getting killed.

Being anxious has no benefits and changes nothing (Luke 12:25), but faith does—it activates heaven on our behalf (Matthew 21:22). Always remember this: *only believe.*

If one of your children has gone astray—*only believe.*

If there is not enough money to meet the needs in your home—*only believe.*

If you have family problems—*only believe.*

If people gossip and spread false rumors about you—*only believe.*

If your husband, co-worker or mother-in-law misunderstands you—*only believe.*

If you are criticized and not appreciated—*only believe.*

If your child is sick and doctors have given up hope—*only believe.*

If you feel uncertain about your children's future—*only believe.*

Let's pray and believe the Lord together for the following needs:

- Pray for the opening of four new training centers before school starts in June.

- Pray for the recruitment of several thousand students.

- Pray that God preserves our freedom to share the Gospel.

Let's honor God with our faith.

Your sister,

Gisela

9 By Faith—Seeing the Big Picture

June 2000

Dear Sister,

Last month our family packed up everything we had and moved to a house that is closer to our new GFA home office. It's a strange feeling to leave the home where our children grew up and where our GFA staff met for 20 years for prayer meetings. However, our ministry grew to a point where we needed a much larger office, and so it was time for us to move as well.

These past few days I have been reading the story of Joseph in the book of Genesis. There are so many important lessons we can learn from his life. For this letter, I would like to choose the lesson about *seeing the big picture*.

Many times our difficult present circumstances overshadow the vision God gave us. It's very easy for this to happen—when our child is sick, someone has said an unkind word to us, our husband comes home after two weeks of field ministry and then has to leave the next morning for a conference, or our expectations are not met by others and we focus our attention on ourselves. Before we know it, our problems, hurts, discouragement and struggles are all we can think of or talk about. Suddenly our eternal perspective and the ministry and vision God has entrusted to us become less important than our personal struggles.

There are times when we doubt that our work has anything to do with real ministry. We might have come to the mission field to join our husband or a Gospel team to go out and win the lost, but our present assignment is kitchen work or cleaning the yard. How can this be part of the fulfillment of our calling?

We are placed under the authority of someone whose decisions don't coincide with our vision. How do we react? Do we fight, murmur in our hearts and walk off the first chance we get, or do we joyfully submit and serve the best we can?

Joseph had to deal with all these circumstances. His personal suffering was overwhelming. The work at Potiphar's house and in the jail didn't resemble anything he saw in his dreams. And as a slave, his life was totally ruled by his owner, who was a heathen. Yet Joseph served with his whole heart, maximum effort and faithfulness.

There are three things that I felt distinguished Joseph the most and allowed him to experience the fulfillment of God's promises:

1. Joseph never doubted God when he suffered all these personal tragedies. When he was thrown in the well, sold by his brothers as a slave, taken to Egypt, falsely accused and sentenced to prison, he could have easily concluded that the God of his fathers had abandoned him. He could have decided that it would be to his advantage to worship the gods of Egypt and seek their favor. Instead he kept his faith alive and trusted and obeyed God in spite of all the things that went wrong. And people around him could see that the Lord was with him (Genesis 39:3, 21).

2. Joseph believed that everything that happened to him fit somewhere into the big picture of God's plan. He certainly didn't understand how, and God chose not to explain it to him until many years later. For 13 years, all he had to go by were the dreams God gave him as a teenager. Because he didn't receive any further revelations, he had no idea when and how the fulfillment would take place. Joseph could have reasoned that his dreams may have resulted from his own imagination and he should forget about them.

Yet because he believed that everything he encountered was a necessary part of God's big picture, he never refused to work hard or submit to authority. And through all this, God trained his character. In addition, the work experience he gained as a slave and overseer was greatly needed when he was appointed to rule Egypt. But most of all, the understanding of God's big picture allowed him to forgive his brothers (Genesis 45:5–8, 50:15–21).

> *Now, therefore, it was not you who sent me here, but God* (Genesis 45:8).

> *And as for you, you meant evil against me, but God meant it for good in order to bring about this present result, to preserve many people alive* (Genesis 50:20).

3. Joseph counted on the sovereignty of God. In his heart he knew that his brothers, Potiphar, the jailer, Pharaoh and all of Egypt were no hindrance for God to fulfill His promises at any time He chose to. That's why Joseph could be at peace in the midst of adversity. Even when the king's cupbearer forgot him for two years, Joseph didn't despair but faithfully carried out his duties, waiting for God's timing.

What if you could see how every part of your life fit in God's big picture and plan? Through the sickness of your child, your faith was forced to grow. The unkind word someone said to you gave you the opportunity to bless in return. When your husband had so little time between his ministry to be at home, you received the honor of laying down your own wishes for the sake of Jesus. And when others didn't meet your expectations, you learned to put your hope in God instead. When you were asked to do kitchen and yard work instead of outreach, God wanted you to practice obedience and submission.

And what you personally learn is just the beginning. Others are influenced and discipled by your life. It may be that the spiritual darkness on your mission field can only be lifted if the Church becomes strong in faith. And you are the Church, along with others.

Everything we face will take on a different meaning, if we choose, like Joseph, to see the big picture. I encourage you to start today.

Please join us in prayer for these needs:

• For the construction of a facility to house all of our GFA printing presses.

- For the purchase of a very large press to print literature in many languages.

- For 15 new Christian print operators to join our staff.

May we yield our lives to the One who purchased us with His own blood.

Your sister,

Gisela

10 Empowered for Ministry

AUGUST 2000

Dear Sister,

Recently I received a wonderful letter from Sister Siny, who works in our Indian GFA office in Tiruvalla, Kerala, and is one of the leaders for our monthly GFA ladies' meeting there. She wrote about the outreach ministry the sisters are doing as an extension of the GFA ladies' meeting.

On weekends they go in teams for prison ministry to share the Gospel with women in five different prisons. They have Bible studies, prayer meetings and times of personal evangelism and counseling with them. Many of the prisoners cry bitterly when they hear about the love of God through the songs, message and skits the sisters share with them. A number of women prisoners have already received Jesus, and their lives have changed dramatically.

Several prison guards told Sister Siny: "What a change has taken place in many of the prisoners' lives! They pray together, read the Bible and ask forgiveness from each other when they say or do something wrong. And they are so obedient to the authorities." By seeing all these positive changes, some of the guards are now beginning to show interest in listening to the Gospel as well.

But there are some guards who won't allow the sisters to talk personally with the prisoners. They also deliberately prevent the women prisoners from listening to our *Athmik Yathra* radio broadcast by keeping the doors locked in the morning until the program is over.

I strongly believe that if we all unite in prayer for them, God will cause these guards to change their attitude. And then Sister Siny will write another letter to report the answer to our prayers, and I will make sure to let you know what happened!

Our life becomes exciting when we permit the Lord to use us to build His kingdom.

Perhaps you think that you would never have the courage to do prison ministry like Sister Siny and her teams, facing hardened criminals and angry prison guards. I haven't asked Sister Siny, but I am certain that she and the sisters in our Tiruvalla office weren't fearless soldiers when they first went out to do such a ministry. However, they went anyway and experienced that God gave them courage and the right words at the moment they needed them. That is His promise when He sends us out into this world on His behalf.

The important thing is that we are available to Him and willing to do whatever ministry He wants to use us for, regardless of our human fear and all the weakness and trembling we may experience at the moment.

When God told Moses in Exodus 3 to go to Pharaoh and lead Israel out of Egypt, Moses listed all his personal problems that he was sure would disqualify him for such a ministry. He said, "I am a nobody; I don't know what to say; no one will believe me or listen to what I say; I am not a good speaker; and I am slow of speech and tongue."

But God wasn't surprised by his weaknesses. He knew them all along. He was not looking for a perfect, capable and fearless leader, only for a willing and obedient one.

Psalm 139 tells us clearly that God knows everything about us, including our thoughts. And Psalm 103:14 leaves us no doubt that God is aware of our insignificance and weaknesses: *"For He Himself knows our frame; He is mindful that we are but dust."*

That's why He gave us the Holy Spirit to empower us for ministry. *"But you shall receive power when the Holy Spirit has come upon you; and you shall be My witnesses. . . . For the promise is for you and your children, and for all who are far off, as many as the Lord our God shall call to Himself"* (Acts 1:8, 2:39).

In this way, we no longer have to go in our own strength to serve God, but in His. All we have to do is to receive what He has promised to every believer. Paul testified in the midst of incredible struggles: *"I can do all things through Him who strengthens me"* (Philippians 4:13).

If God has made all the provisions to empower us for ministry, we can no longer use our weakness and fear as an excuse not to serve Him.

All there is left for us to do is to go in faith and believe His promises, and we will be amazed to see what God can do through our lives by His power. Yes, we may still be shy and experience human fear, but our faith will overcome it because we no longer focus on our weakness. Instead, we count on His strength that works through us.

My dear Sister, whatever God gives you to do, say "yes" to Him and trust Him. He will always stand by you.

Let us pray now specifically for the prison ministry of our sisters in Tiruvalla:

- Pray for all the women prisoners who have received Christ, that they will grow in their faith and stand firm in their decision to follow Jesus.

- Pray for the salvation of the guards and those prisoners who have rejected the Gospel message.

- Pray that the guards will allow the prisoners to hear the *Athmik Yathra* radio broadcast and permit personal evangelism.

- Pray for our sisters in Tiruvalla, that God will use their lives in all they do for Him.

If your GFA or Believers Church ladies' meeting is involved in outreach ministry, it would be wonderful if you could tell me about it. I would like to share more stories and prayer requests from our GFA sisters' mission work in my letter to you. That way our lives will be drawn much closer to each other and our prayers for one another will be more specific. You can send the information to your regional or country office, and they will translate it if necessary and forward it to me.

May the Lord bless you. I look forward to writing to you again.

Your sister,

Gisela

11

Don't Allow Your Emotions to Make Ministry Decisions

OCTOBER 2000

Dear Sister,

Last month my mother turned 86 years old. I am thankful that she is doing well, and I hope to visit her soon. Sometimes she feels sad that I live so far away. I would appreciate you remembering her in your prayers.

There is something I have been thinking about a lot lately. I have observed in the lives of many who started out to serve the Lord that their commitment to their calling is very fragile. When the initial excitement is over, a co-worker offends them, they disagree with an assignment or difficulties come, they want to leave the battle. I believe with all my heart that God wishes for all of us to fulfill our calling. Practically, this means that we need to be faithful—to whatever call we received—for the next 20, 30 or 50 years.

I'd like to think that you are doing well. But just in case you struggle, this letter is for you. Perhaps you not only feel discouraged, but it is impossible for you to imagine surviving on your mission field even another month. You have faced so many difficulties and personal struggles that you have decided to leave the team or you have convinced your husband to move back to the place you both came from. All these circumstances have heavily influenced your emotions. You feel lonely, you are overwhelmed with demands and you miss your former lifestyle and friends.

But what about the call of God you received? Didn't you set out to serve Jesus for the rest of your life? What happened?

You allowed your emotions to make ministry decisions!

If we want to survive in the ministry, it is important for us to understand two things about our emotions:

1. How powerful they are; and

2. The place they *must* have in our lives as followers of Christ, so they will not become a hindrance to our calling.

God gave us emotions when He created us in His own image. It's truly a wonderful gift that enables us to experience life, enjoy the beauty of nature, build intimate relationships with others and respond to our God with our heart. We are capable of feeling and expressing love, joy, peace, tenderness, kindness, compassion and gratitude—as well as hate, sadness, fear, pain, discouragement and rejection.

God created each of us with a body, soul and spirit. His original design was that our soul and body be governed by our spirit, which would be in total subjection to our Creator. That way our emotions (which are part of our soul) would be a blessing to ourselves and others, and they would never overpower us and dictate our actions in life. Obedience to God would be the only deciding factor for everything we did.

However, with the fall of man, God's order got messed up. Man's spirit was no longer in subjection to God, and for the most part, our soul and body took over the leadership of our life. The appetites of our body and the surge of our emotions became so powerful that we followed them and disregarded God's Word.

Think about it: Jealousy becomes the reason for spreading false rumors . . . greed leads to dishonesty, theft and robbery . . . bitterness, anger and hatred without restraint end up in destruction and murder . . . rape and adultery are the result of gratifying selfish emotions.

Jesus came to restore what was lost. When we were born again, the Holy Spirit took up His residence in our spirit to empower us to once again bring our whole being—spirit, soul and body—under subjection to God. God's intent is that from now on, our spirit lives in total obedience to the Holy Spirit and rules our soul and body. If that happens, we will act in obedience to God's Word and not to our emotions or the demands of our body.

It will not happen by itself. Our body and soul, with all its emotions, have been in charge of our lives for so long that we find it difficult not to obey them. The apostle Paul tells us what to do to succeed in bringing them to the obedience of Christ:

> *I urge you . . . to present your bodies a living and holy sacrifice, acceptable to God. . . . Be transformed by the renewing of your mind* (Romans 12:1–2).

We are destroying speculations and every lofty thing raised up against the knowledge of God, and we are taking every thought captive to the obedience of Christ (2 Corinthians 10:5).

Set your mind on the things above, not on the things that are on earth (Colossians 3:2).

We must declare open war on the demands of our body and soul if they act contrary to the will of God for our lives!

Our obedience to our calling *must* overrule our emotions. If we don't learn this, sooner or later we will walk away. Jesus was able to steadfastly set His face toward Jerusalem to face death on the cross because His will and emotions were completely surrendered to the will of God.

Our God does not expect us to be void of feelings; otherwise, He would have created us that way. However, He wants us to get to the place where we choose obedience to His Word and calling above our tears and hurts. Only then can He fulfill His purpose through our lives.

We must count on His grace that is sufficient, even if circumstances don't change. Paul testified to this in 2 Corinthians 12:8–10. Dear Sister, we will find our greatest fulfillment not in being led by our emotions, but in doing the will of God!

Let us pray and believe God together for these needs:

• For grace for all our sisters who struggle with their commitment to their calling.

- For seven new radio broadcasts that will go on the air by the beginning of next year.

With love and
prayers,

Gisela

12

His Name Is Wonderful

Dear Sister,

I am excited about the month of December. First of all, it's Christmas—and I love to celebrate the birth of Jesus together with our family and God's people around the world. Second, our children will be coming home for two weeks. I have not seen them since May. Both of them are doing further studies at our ABS in India. In addition, Daniel is traveling quite a bit and helping our brothers on different GFA mission fields, while Sarah is serving at the ABS as the girls' warden together with her friend from Nagaland, India. I am deeply grateful that we have the privilege to serve the Lord as a family.

Because it will be Christmas soon, I want to share with you a little about the gift of God we have received in Jesus.

His name is wonderful. Just before I sat down to write this letter, I listened to a beautiful Gospel song that you may know as well: "His Name Is Wonderful." The song refers to the prophetic Scripture in the book of Isaiah that describes to us the coming Savior of the world with these words:

And His name will be called **Wonderful Counselor, Mighty God, Eternal Father, Prince of Peace** *(Isaiah 9:6).*

There are many other names in the Bible that give us even more details about who Jesus is. Here are just a few of them:

- *Immanuel* (Matthew 1:23), which means *"God with us."*

- *The Way, the Truth and the Life* (John 14:6).

- *Rock* (1 Corinthians 10:4).

- *The same yesterday and today, yes and forever* (Hebrews 13:8).

- *The Author and Perfecter of our faith* (Hebrews 12:2).

- *Lord of all* (Acts 10:36).

- *The Good Shepherd* (John 10:11).

- *Deliverer* (Romans 11:26).

- *Healer* (Matthew 9:35).

- *"There is salvation in no one else; for* **there is no other name** *under heaven that has been given among men,* **by which we must be saved"** (Acts 4:12).

What is God trying to tell us with all these names?

That He is very well aware of all our struggles, failures, fears, confusion, suffering and the persecution we may face for the Gospel.

That He does not scold, condemn, revoke our calling or turn His back on us when we are discouraged, weak or overcome by failure.

That He has assessed every one of our struggles in life—and He has provided a perfect solution for each of them.

That He sent His solution as a gift 2,000 years ago: Jesus, His Son.

There is not a problem or struggle in our life or ministry where Jesus is not the answer. When we feel lonely or forsaken by all, He is our *Emmanuel*. In our confusion, He is our *Counselor*. When we are in the midst of a storm, He is our *Rock*. When we don't know what direction to go, He is the *Way*. When our heart is troubled, He is the *Prince of Peace*. When we are surrounded by opposition, He is the *Mighty God* and our *Deliverer*. When we are frightened by all the changes around us, He remains the *same*—yesterday, today and forever. When we are overwhelmed and overburdened in the ministry, He is the *Good Shepherd* who leads us to a place of refreshment. Even if death approaches us, He is the *Resurrection and the Life*.

God made it easy for us to recognize where we need to turn to with our problems by putting name labels on His Son Jesus. But sadly, we don't read the name labels, or we ignore them and try to find our answers in all the wrong places.

God's way is so simple: Don't ignore or doubt the name labels that God put on Jesus. Find the one that spells out the solution to your problem. And then believe with all your heart that He indeed is your answer. As you put your faith in Him, He will fulfill each promise that is contained in His name.

Celebrate this Christmas by getting to know who Jesus is. Take time to go through your Bible and look at all the wonderful names of Jesus you can find. Write them down on a sheet of paper, pray and think deeply about the meaning of each one of them and then apply them to your situation. Perhaps you can do this also as a group in your ladies meeting. The more you discover who Jesus is, the more your joy and faith will increase, and Christmas will take on a much deeper meaning.

Dear Sister, do you see how precious you are in God's sight by all He gave you when He sent Jesus to become your Savior?

Let us take time to remember God's love for us and thank Him for:

- Sending Jesus and for our salvation.

- All that is ours in Jesus.

- Our calling to serve Him.

- The privilege to suffer, give up something or face rejection for His name's sake.

- All the blessings, protection and care we received from Him during this past year.

- His promises that remain the same for this coming year.

May the peace and joy of the Lord be with you as you celebrate Christmas and step out into the new year.

With love and
prayers,

Gisela

13 Don't Excuse Cultural Behavior

Dear Sister,

I am writing this letter to you while traveling to India to take part in our first GFA leaders' Family Conference. I am looking forward to meeting everyone, and I will be sure to tell you more about the event in my next letter.

Our GFA family is made up of brothers and sisters from many different countries, races and people groups. It's exciting to attend some of our larger conferences to see the many different faces and hear people worshiping the Lord in their native languages. It's almost like a glimpse of our future in heaven, when we will be part of the great multitude described in Revelation 7:9 that will worship the Lamb.

Having such a diversity of people in our GFA family is a great blessing as well as a challenge. The blessing is that we can draw from a variety of strengths from one another and work among many different people groups at the same time. The challenge is to accept each other in humility and love and to grow together in unity and service to our King.

Generally, each one of us is the product of the family and society in which we grew up. This means that we learned our way of life, our thinking, our behavior and our value system from those around us. We accept these standards as normal or even superior to those of others, and we automatically evaluate and judge everyone and everything we encounter by what we have been taught.

There are deep, ingrained thought and behavioral patterns in each society that stand out and characterize its people. Though not all individuals may exhibit every one of these trademarks, most people will have them, at least to some degree.

Some of these outstanding features are positive in light of the biblical standard—for example, generosity, hospitality, hard work, being easily adaptable and loyalty—but others are not: jealousy, feelings that are easily hurt, taking revenge at all costs, outbursts of anger, fighting for one's way, disloyalty, dishonesty for personal gain and pride in social status.

As followers of Christ, we are called to represent Jesus to this world through our lives: *"Because as He is, so also are we in this world. . . . Therefore, we are ambassadors for Christ"* (1 John 4:17; 2 Corinthians 5:20).

Our calling to be an exact representation of Jesus in the way we think, act and live may, in many areas, conflict severely with the behavior pattern of our society and culture. What should our response be? How should we resolve this problem?

Many Christians simply ignore or justify their unbiblical behavior with the excuse that their anger or tendency to fight is simply part of their culture and therefore acceptable. In their perception, this character trait is nothing serious, and so they never make a genuine attempt to change. Even when the Holy Spirit convicts them of their un-Christlike behavior, they don't respond with sincerity. In reality, their cultural heritage takes priority over their calling.

This attitude has seriously hurt the cause of Christ. The world around us is not able to see a clear representation of Christ in our lives, but rather a mixture of Christianity and culturally unbiblical behavior. It makes the Gospel look weak and seemingly unable to fulfill 2 Corinthians 5:17—*"Therefore if any man is in Christ, he is a new creature; the old things passed away; behold, new things have come."*

The sad thing is that in the Lord's work it has become normal to hear statements like these:

> We don't take Bible school students from XX people group, because they always fight and cause divisions. . . . Be careful if you put anyone from XX background into leadership; no matter how loyal he appears to be, one day he will stab you in the back. . . . Don't be fooled by the gentleness of a Christian worker from XX place— these people always build cliques with their own kind and cause a lot of problems.

The apostle Paul faced similar problems on his mission fields. In his letter to Titus, Paul gave clear instructions about how Titus should deal with converts in Crete, whose cultural behavior conflicted with Scripture:

One of themselves, a prophet of their own, said, "Cretans are always liars, evil beasts, lazy gluttons." This testimony is true. For this cause reprove them severely that they may be sound in the faith (Titus 1:12–13).

Paul didn't give these new Christians an excuse for their "normal" Cretan lifestyle, nor did he say that it was impossible for them to change. He obviously believed that these people could become a clear and powerful testimony for Christ.

We must recognize that we are living in a fallen world, corrupted by sin. God does not want us to despise the culture and people we are part of. But He expects us to make a careful evaluation of the thinking and behavior patterns of our society in the light of Scripture. As followers of Christ, God's Word must be the final authority for our life—in any culture—for us to be able to accurately represent Christ.

For the sake of Jesus, let us not be blind to the things in our culture that contradict God's Word. Instead, let us become a testimony for the transforming power of the Gospel.

Please join us in prayer for GFA's new Christian TV program that went on the air for the first time on December 24, 2000:

- Pray for the production of quality programs.

- Pray that the Gospel message will come through clearly and in a powerful way.

- Pray for a huge listening audience.

- Pray for the production of different language programs.

- Pray for the Holy Spirit to touch hearts and draw people to Jesus.

May the Lord bless you and let you realize that He is always with you.

Your sister,

Gisela

14 Do Your Children Know What You Live For?

Dear Sister,

Time is flying by so fast since I returned home in February from my trip to India.

Our leaders' Family Conference in Kerala, India, turned out to be one of the most important meetings we have ever had as a fast-growing movement. You see, for the first time, the wives and children of our leaders from India and other countries had the opportunity to meet each other and to learn about the ministry as a whole. The children had their own exciting programs, while the sisters attended the regular teaching sessions. The conference centered on the theme "Training in Godliness."

All the sisters and small children stayed in our ABS girls' hostel, and the students who volunteered to work during their Christmas vacation did a wonderful job looking after them and making them feel at home.

During the afternoons, the sisters had several separate sessions where they discussed how to implement in their personal life and in their family the things they were learning: the type of character a leader's or pastor's wife should have; what the family life of a servant of God should be; and what it means for a wife to be one with her husband, both spiritually and practically, as co-laborers in the ministry.

Sister Siny and Sister Angel from our GFA office organized and headed up the ladies' program. They enlisted other sisters from the office and the ABS for putting on skits, leading worship and coordinating morning devotions and family prayer. Each day some of our leaders' wives or single sisters shared prayer requests from their ministry and mission fields. It really helped us get to know each other and learn how we could remember each other in prayer even after the conference was over.

My part in the ladies' program was teaching on Christian family life and raising children based on biblical principles.

One of the highlights of the conference was the opportunity to build relationships and to see the families of our leaders grow in their understanding of what it means to serve the Lord together.

Another was the children's drama presentation of reaching the lost of Asia during our closing program. They dressed up representing different tribes and people groups, as well as problems of society. Then they showed how Jesus comes to help as GFA takes the Gospel to the unreached.

At the end of the conference, everyone was asked to fill out a questionnaire. The questions were about our personal relationship with the Lord, our ministry involvement, things we learned at the conference and decisions we made during the week. No one was required to sign his or her name, which helped us all feel more free in sharing our hearts. The questionnaires will help our leaders evaluate the effectiveness of the conference and learn the issues that need to be addressed in the future.

I am aware that my letter goes to many sisters who didn't have the opportunity to attend this conference. And perhaps when you read this, you wish that there would be a meeting like this in your area.

Our GFA leadership is very much aware of the importance of teaching and strengthening the families of our missionaries and the believers in the churches. It's not just the sisters who could use encouragement and instruction—there are also thousands of children and young people who grow up within our GFA family and in Believers Churches. They need to know the Lord personally and what it means to live for Him and put Him first in their lives.

Your own children, as well, will sooner or later make decisions for their futures. Ask yourself if, based on what they observe in your life and in your family life, they would desire to serve the Lord too.

Do your children really know what you and your husband live for? Do you take time to help them understand about GFA, the vision we have for the unreached, the values we hold and what is happening on the mission fields? Do they feel that they are an important part of the ministry with their prayers, their testimony and what they do to help get the Gospel out?

Do they feel privileged to grow up in the family of servants of God? Do you instill in them, with your attitude, your words and your example, a longing for the things of God—or for the things of the world? If they were to choose a profession or job today, would they go for money, position, security and honor—or would they seek the Lord's face to find His will for their lives?

Dear Sister, please don't wait for a conference to come to your place to help your children—or the children and young people in Believers Churches—understand what it means to live for Jesus, to choose Him above all else and to have a heart for missions. Show them the way with your life and teach them what you have learned yourself. You do not necessarily have to stand in front of a class and deliver a lecture. Often the most significant teaching is done during a *normal,* one-on-one conversation. Pray for the Lord to give you opportunities to help draw these children and young people toward Him.

Our GFA leaders will arrange more regional conferences to strengthen our families in the days to come. Maybe one of them will be near you. I, too, will be traveling more this year to share in ladies' meetings. Perhaps I will meet you.

Please pray with us for the following needs:

- The ongoing outreach to the earthquake survivors in Gujarat, India.

- The new GFA graduates who are beginning their ministries.

- The children and young people in GFA and Believers Churches, that they will grow up serving Jesus.

I love you in Jesus,

Gisela

15 Fill Your Heart with the Word of God

JUNE 2001

Dear Sister,

This morning when I sat down at my kitchen table to write this letter to you, I wondered what I could share with you that would encourage you in your walk with the Lord and in your ministry. There is so little, or nothing, that I know about your life and the things you are concerned about. But then I remembered that the same Holy Spirit who lives in you is in me as well, and I can trust Him to guide me to write the words that will help you.

I remember times in my personal life as well as in my service to the Lord when I went through struggles, discouragement and hurt. Some of it I caused myself; the rest was because of other people. But in either case, the most difficult thing was that there was no one I could talk to about it. I felt so alone and didn't know what to do.

During those times, different Scripture portions became very real and alive to me. I would read them over and over to myself, until I could cling to them in faith and with all my heart. And I experienced a wonderful thing: God stood by the Word I held onto and brought me safely through every time. Now as I look back, each of those Scriptures has a personal story of God's faithfulness attached to it. Today I want to share a few of these Scriptures with you.

God knows exactly how much I can bear: *"For He Himself knows our frame; He is mindful that we are but dust"* (Psalm 103:14).

This Scripture tells me that my Creator has calculated my strength, and He knows how fragile I am in my physical as well as in my spiritual life. He will never overload me or permit trials to come my way that would destroy my faith in Him. Therefore, I can trust Him, even if I don't understand what is going on or why some of these things are happening in my life.

My heavenly Father is aware of my need: *". . . Thou dost understand my thought from afar"* (Psalm 139:2). *"Do not be anxious . . . for your heavenly Father knows that you need all these things"* (Matthew 6:31–32).

God as my Father knows not only the needs I have in my daily life, such as clothing, food, shelter, health and protection—He also knows the deepest yearnings of my heart: the understanding, love, acceptance, comfort and fulfillment I long for in my marriage . . . the strength and endurance I need as a mother . . . the friendship, fellowship and encouragement I so much desire at my lonely place of ministry.

The moment my heart receives the truth that "my heavenly Father *knows* that I need all these things," my anxiety, fear, desperation and tears will be replaced by deep peace, joy and trust. Then, even if I can't see the answer yet, I know for sure that my Father not only knows my needs but will meet them as He promised.

God has not forgotten me: *"How precious also are Thy thoughts to me, O God! How vast is the sum of them! If I should count them, they would outnumber the sand"* (Psalm 139:17–18).

This means God is continually thinking about me, even right now in the midst of my struggle. And His thoughts about me are not angry or impatient, but precious and loving. In fact, I mean so much to Him that He can't stop thinking about me. That knowledge fills me with joy and thankfulness. And I realize I am no longer hurting, that those whom I considered my friends have forgotten me or don't care about me.

What I really want to tell you today is this: You need to fill your heart with God's Word.

Our very survival as Christians depends on it: *"Man shall not live on bread alone, but on every word that proceeds out of the mouth of God"* (Matthew 4:4).

It produces faith in our hearts, which then enables us to receive from God: *"So faith comes from hearing, and hearing by the word of Christ"* (Romans 10:17).

It is part of our armor to defeat the enemy: *". . . and the sword of the Spirit, which is the word of God"* (Ephesians 6:17).

It shows us the way we must go: *"Thy word is a lamp to my feet, and a light to my path"* (Psalm 119:105).

It's our God-given instruction on how to live as Christians: *"All Scripture is inspired by God and profitable for teaching, for reproof, for correction, for training in righteousness"* (2 Timothy 3:16).

And there is so much more.

How can you do this?

- Read God's Word daily and ask the Holy Spirit to reveal it to you.

- Take notes on what you learn at church or when you read the Bible.

- Meditate on a Scripture by thinking about it over and over again.

- Learn important Bible verses by heart.

My dear Sister, let us pray for one another, that we will live with all our hearts for our King.

Your sister,

Gisela

16 What Does It Take to Lead Others?

AUGUST 2001

Dear Sister,

The first two-and-a-half weeks of June were some of the most exciting I have ever had in North India. We held our first four Sisters' Seminars in Delhi, Bilaspur and Nagpur. Each seminar lasted three days, and nearly 900 sisters attended from the states of Gujarat, Rajasthan, Haryana, Punjab, Himachal Pradesh, Jammu and Kashmir, Uttar Pradesh, Jharkhand, Bihar, Chhattisgarh, Madhya Pradesh and Maharashtra.

The Lord answered many prayers by giving us rain at all three conference sites, and the climate was very pleasant. For many of the sisters, it was their first time traveling away from their homes and attending a meeting of this kind. They very much enjoyed the fellowship and were encouraged to find out that they are part of a large family that prays and cares for them.

Together, we studied what it means to follow Jesus and how we can practically apply what the Bible teaches about marriage, family, raising children and serving the Lord. For me, it was such a joy to observe the eagerness and sincerity of the sisters as they learned new things and made decisions in the light of what God showed them.

Each afternoon and evening, we had "feedback sessions" led by sisters from our GFA staff and some of the pastors who had brought the sisters from their districts. Each group discussed the lessons, and every sister had a chance to share her personal response to it. In fact, we received stacks of letters from our sisters, telling us about the changes they were making in their lives as a result of the seminars. The last session ended with a time of prayer, dedication and submission to Jesus.

Personally, I felt very blessed that the Lord gave me the privilege to be part of these meetings. It was wonderful to finally meet so many of my sisters to whom I write these letters! Now I feel even closer to all of them, and my vision for our GFA women's ministry has grown a lot.

I am very thankful to our regional coordinators, Brother Simon and Brother Lalachen, for arranging these meetings; the sisters who translated for me; the Bible school students and their teachers from Ambala and Bilaspur who blessed us with songs and skits; and the many other brothers and sisters who worked so hard to provide for all the needs of the participants.

After the meetings were over, several of our pastors' and leaders' wives told me that they had decided to teach the things

they learned in the seminar to the sisters in their areas and to the ladies of our Believers Churches.

It is indeed my prayer and vision that eventually all our GFA and Believers Church sisters will teach the principles of God's Word regarding Christian marriage, family and service to the ladies in our churches. If that happens, and if the men will receive similar training from our pastors, the foundation of each church will be greatly strengthened. And, as a result, our pastors' and believers' families will have a powerful testimony in their communities.

Dear Sister, with all my heart I want you to be effective in teaching others. That's why I want to share with you the most important principle in teaching spiritual things: You must live and model with your life whatever you teach. Whatever you don't live, you cannot teach others. It will not work. The reason is this: Only that which is life in you will produce life in others.

In whatever area God is able to change and train you, in that area you can help others to learn. The more you spare yourself from submitting to God and learning what He is trying to teach you, the less useful you will be in His work.

> You cannot challenge others to go wherever God sends them . . . if you refuse to go with your husband (or with a team, if you are single) to a mission field that takes you more than 100 kilometers away from your relatives.

> You cannot tell someone to step out in faith and trust God . . . if you demand that your husband or field leadership first provide all the securities—a regular income, a comfortable house, your children's education—before you are willing to move to a pioneer field.

You cannot ask a sister to fully join and support her husband in his calling . . . if you yourself haven't done it.

Especially if your husband is in leadership, both of you are called to be an example of what it means to follow Christ without reservation and with all your heart. You cannot teach and lead others beyond the commitment you have yourself. God is not looking for perfection in us, but He looks for sincerity and a willingness to learn and practice what we intend to teach others.

By no means do I want to discourage you from teaching others or tell you to wait a few more years until you've learned it all. Teach others everything you have learned and received from the Lord so far, and expand your teaching as you respond to God's dealing with your own heart.

Let us pray together and ask for God's blessings on:

- All the sisters who attended the seminars, that He will give them grace to apply what they learned.

- The pastors and students of our 88 new home Bible schools, which are opening within the next few months.

- The next four Sisters' Seminars to be held during September in India and Nepal.

I am thankful to serve the Lord together with you.

Your sister,

Gisela

17 Facing Your Problems with Prayer

OCTOBER 2001

Dear Sister,

Do you remember the jail ministry of our Indian GFA sisters in Tiruvalla, Kerala? I shared with you a letter from Sister Siny a little over a year ago. In this letter, she wrote how some of the prison guards were not allowing them to talk to the ladies in the jail and preventing the inmates from listening to our *Athmik Yathra* radio broadcast. The specific prayer request in our August 2000 letter was that God would change the hearts of those guards who were opposing the ministry of our sisters.

I just received the following update from Sister Siny, and I know it will encourage you to find out how God answered our prayers:

Starting this year, we are conducting a worship service in this particular prison. In the worship service we have time for intercessory prayer. So we are praying for every individual request.

Four months ago, after the worship service, one of the inmates came to me and said, "Our Matron [police officer who is looking after the prisoners, and a strong Hindu lady] wants your prayers."

This woman was opposing us to do the ministry and did not even like us to visit this prison. So I went and talked to her very personally. She was suffering from so many diseases (kidney problems, high blood pressure, piles, asthma and muscular pain) and had a lot of problems in her family. So I shared the Gospel with her, and we together as a team prayed. Also, we have given the assurance to pray for her continuously. We shared this request to everybody in the office and they were praying for it.

When we visited this prison the following month, she was healed from most of the diseases. She used to take a lot of medicines, but now she believes that God will heal her completely.

These days she is very happy with our team. She is making all the arrangements for us to conduct the program. All the police officers of this prison are very kind to us and allowing us to talk to the prisoners. They are requesting us not only to pray for their own needs, but are also sharing the problems and prayer needs of the prisoners.

Pray that the Lord may change these guards' hearts and that they would become radical followers of Christ.

This letter is a wonderful testimony of how God changes difficult situations when we pray in faith.

All of us face problems regardless of how spiritually minded we are. It is a normal part of living in a fallen world plagued with sin, sickness and death.

Our salvation and the Holy Spirit's living in us do not eliminate all difficulties and suffering from our lives. In fact, we may face additional problems, such as trials allowed by God to test the quality of our faith, persecution from unbelievers and attacks from Satan, who seeks to destroy our life, testimony and ministry.

The most important decision is what we are going to do about our problems. We usually talk or worry about our impossible situations and feel sorry for ourselves. Sometimes we are so discouraged or hurt that we let days and even weeks go by before we seriously look for a biblical solution.

But regardless of the source from which our problems originate, we cannot afford to sit and wallow in our hurt. As children of the living God, we must rise up and overcome.

The Bible gives us very specific instructions on how we should deal with difficult situations:

- Suffering: *"Is anyone among you suffering? Let him **pray**"* (James 5:13).

- Sickness: *"Is anyone among you sick? Let him call for the elders of the church, and let them **pray** over him, anointing him with oil in the name of the Lord; and the **prayer** offered in faith will restore the one who is sick, and the Lord will raise him up"* (James 5:14–15).

- Persecution: *"But I say to you, love your enemies, and **pray** for those who persecute you"* (Matthew 5:44).

- Attacks and temptations of Satan: *"Keep watching and **praying**, that you may not enter into temptation; the spirit is willing, but the flesh is weak"* (Matthew 26:41).

- Needs in our life and ministry: *"Be anxious for nothing, but in everything by **prayer** and supplication with thanksgiving let your requests be made known to God"* (Philippians 4:6).

It is obvious that every time we face a problem, God wants us to first come to Him in prayer. If we follow this instruction, we will save ourselves much heartache, tears and frustration. Bringing our problems to Him shows our trust in our heavenly Father and proves our dependence on Him. It gives Him the opportunity to work on our behalf and answer our prayers far beyond our expectations.

Remember, taking our difficulties to Him is always a shortcut to the very best solution.

We must come in faith. Just bringing our problems to God is not enough for Him to do something about it. Unless there is faith in our hearts, nothing will change.

And everything you ask in prayer, believing, you shall receive (Matthew 21:22).

Let us pray in faith together for:

- The 88 new home Bible schools GFA is starting this year. Several of them are for sisters.

- God to raise up leaders for our Believers Church women's ministry.

May God's grace be with you as you serve Him.

Your sister,

Gisela

18 Longing for the Coming of Jesus

DECEMBER 2001

Dear Sister,

I am amazed how fast this year has gone by. It will be almost Christmas by the time you get my letter. This year our family will spend Christmas in India, because our leaders' Family Conference will take place during the last week of December.

In September and October, I taught at four more Sisters' Seminars in Nepal and in the Indian states of West Bengal, Andhra Pradesh and Tamil Nadu. Thank you for praying for these meetings. Each one was exciting and unique at the same time. I am so thankful that in each place the ladies who attended made many personal decisions to practically apply the things they learned to their families and ministries.

The Lord made it possible for Sister Heidi from our GFA USA office to be with me on this trip and to share with the sisters what God has taught her in her life and service to Him. We enjoyed traveling together and especially meeting the hundreds of sisters from the different mission fields.

We came back with so many wonderful memories and stories from each place we visited. Perhaps our most "overwhelming" adventure was the seminar in Nepal.

Our leaders invited between 250–300 sisters, but close to 600 showed up. Some of them came from the interior parts of Nepal, walking and traveling by bus from between three to nine days. It was amazing to see all these ladies squeezed into a hall that was built to hold only 300. No doubt we experienced very close fellowship with each other!

After the last session, all these dear sisters came to the platform to express their love for Sister Heidi and me by squeezing, hugging and kissing us goodbye. We still laugh and talk about it with joy.

In Andhra Pradesh, the Lord arranged a wonderful surprise for me. My daughter, Sarah, arrived from the ABS in Kerala to be with us during the last two seminars. She said she came to support my ministry. I enjoyed her visit so much, and now I miss her even more than before.

As I write this letter, in my mind I can see many faces before me of the sisters we met from Bhutan, Sikkim, Nepal and all the other places. I am so thankful that the Lord has linked our lives together through calling us to reach the unreached of Asia with the Gospel. What a privilege!

In this Christmas letter, I would like to share with you a few thoughts about the coming of our Savior. Perhaps you may want to reflect on it during your personal time with the Lord.

Ever since the fall of man, people have waited and longed for the coming of the promised Savior. Separated from the living God, mankind was ravaged by the devil and the consequences of sin. Sickness, suffering, destruction and death had replaced the peace, joy and fellowship men had once enjoyed with the living God. Now their only hope was that someday God would fulfill His Word and send the Deliverer who would take away their sin and restore them back to their Creator.

In every generation that followed Adam, those who believed in this promise hoped and prayed that the Messiah would come during their lifetime.

And finally, the longing of all those generations was fulfilled when Jesus the Savior was born 2,000 years ago. Luke records for us the rejoicing of Simeon and Anna when the baby Jesus was brought into the temple by His parents.

> *Then he [Simeon] took Him into his arms, and blessed God, and said: "Now Lord, Thou dost let Thy bondservant depart in peace, according to Thy word; for mine eyes have seen Thy salvation, which Thou hast prepared in the presence of all peoples, a light of revelation to the Gentiles, and the glory of Thy people Israel" (Luke 2:28–32).*

> *At that very moment she [Anna] came up and began giving thanks to God, and continued to speak of Him to all those who were looking for the redemption of Jerusalem (Luke 2:38).*

Now we who belong to Him once again wait and long for His return. After Jesus accomplished our salvation He went back to the Father, giving us this promise: *"I will come again, and receive you to Myself; that where I am, there you may be also"* (John 14:3). This promise fills us with great joy and expectation, and it gives us strength when we go through trials and persecution.

The apostle John ends the book of Revelation with the renewed promise of Jesus: *"Yes, I am coming quickly,"* and the response of the Church, which is us: *"Amen. Come, Lord Jesus"* (Revelation 22:20).

I invite you to celebrate Christmas this year by letting the Lord know:

- How thankful you are for His fulfilling the promise of the Father and becoming your Savior.

- How much you love Him and long for His return.

- That He may use your life, without reservation, to take His name to those multitudes who still sit in darkness, longing and waiting for a Deliverer.

My dear Sister, may God's presence and peace be real to you this Christmas and every day of the coming year.

I love you in Jesus,

Gisela

19 Family Conference and Sisters' Seminar

February 2002

Dear Sister,

I am writing this letter to you from Kerala, India. Just yesterday, I finished the last Sisters' Seminar during this trip. It was at the ABS, and it turned out to be a Sisters' and Brothers' Seminar. Our seminary leadership felt it would be beneficial for the personal life and future ministry of all the students to attend these classes on the Christian family. We had 15 sessions over three days. The sisters were happy with the things they learned, and some of the brothers commented: "We got married, became fathers and raised children—all within three days."

Our leaders' Family Conference took place from December 23–31. It was wonderful to meet so many of our leaders, their wives and children from all the Asian countries in which we work. Many of our brothers and sisters traveled for days to get here. Our Myanmar delegates were on the road 17 days.

The theme of the conference was the prayer of Jesus from John 17:21—*"that they may all be one."* And indeed, we all felt this oneness and love for one another as we celebrated Christmas together, learned from God's Word, listened to exciting reports from the mission fields and ended the conference with a watch night service. The sessions were translated into several languages so everyone could understand. During our separate ladies' meetings, eight different translations took place as the ladies sat together in language groups throughout the auditorium. It was an enormous task to coordinate, house, feed and look after 1,154 conference participants. But everything went very smoothly, thanks to the hard work and dedication of our staff and 143 student volunteers, who sacrificed their Christmas vacation to serve the Lord and our leaders during the conference.

More than 280 children took part in the conference, and they enjoyed an excellent children's program for all age groups. Brother Saji, our ABS Sunday School Ministry coordinator, taught them along with our students. The children enjoyed "their" conference so much that many of them didn't want to go back home; and all of them were planning to come back to the next conference. The beautiful thing was that many of our leaders' children gave their hearts to Jesus, and 20 of them made serious decisions to serve the Lord as missionaries when they grow up.

For two days after the conference ended, we were busy saying goodbye to all the dear brothers and sisters who were leaving to go back to their mission fields.

On January 3, I traveled to the Indian state of Karnataka for our Sisters' Seminar. Approximately 89 of our pastors' wives and single sisters working in team ministry took part in the meetings. I felt very blessed to be able to spend these few days with them. I learned that the Lord used our five sisters' teams to start six fellowships that are now Believers Churches. Right after our seminar ended, the students returned from their Christmas vacation, so I also had the opportunity to meet most of them before I left.

I am so encouraged by all the Lord has done these past few years through the ministry of our Karnataka training center graduates. This state is known as a very hard and difficult mission field. I remember so well that when our leaders first decided to open a training center in this state, they were told by every Christian organization that it was nearly impossible to get any Kannada students. None of the existing schools had more than two or three. Believers around the world began to pray with us, and when the school opened in December of 1993, we had 37 students from Karnataka state. It was clearly a miracle.

During this trip I also learned that there are currently 130 brothers and 55 sisters, all from Karnataka, who are studying in our main training center near Mangalore. Because of the many young people who want to serve the Lord, we had to open a branch-training center in Bijapur with 76 students and three home Bible schools with a combined student body of 49. There are still many more, especially sisters, who have applied to come for training, but we don't have enough room to take them.

In the meantime, we have 260 missionaries on the field in Karnataka. All but 10 or 15 of them are graduates from our training center. They have already established 136 churches and are doing church-planting work in 445 mission stations. We also have a Kannada radio broadcast that is heard four days a week. Brother Peter, our Karnataka leader, has been doing this broadcast for eight years. Many of our students were saved through this radio program, and God is using this broadcast to soften the hearts of the people toward the Gospel.

Three days after returning from Karnataka, our next Sisters' Seminar took place in Trivandrum, Kerala. It was held in connection with our Believers Church state convention, and 360 pastors and approximately 289 sisters took part in this three-day meeting. During the daytime we had our separate Sisters' Seminar, and in the evenings we, along with all the pastors, attended meetings that were open to the public. My husband preached a salvation message to a crowd of 7,000 on the first night, 12,000 on the second and 15,000 people on the last night. Each evening during the invitation, at least 90 percent of the audience made decisions to receive Christ. I wish you could have been there to witness these people calling upon the name of Jesus for salvation; many were loudly weeping.

A very sad thing happened right after the last evening meeting. Three of our believers who attended the convention were killed on their way home when a speeding bus hit their jeep. One of the ladies who was killed has three children. Please pray for the families that were left behind.

In just a few days I will pack my bags to travel home. I am thankful to God for the time He gave me to be with our sisters and students at these different meetings. My sincere hope is that He has encouraged them to walk more closely with Jesus and serve Him with all their hearts.

Please pray and believe with us for our Believers Church ministry in Karnataka:

- For a mighty move of God in Karnataka.

- For God to empower our missionaries and students to establish churches in all 7,000 taluks of this state.

- For anointing and strength for Brother Peter as he does the Kannada broadcast.

- For grace and wisdom for Sister Beena, our ABS graduate who is in charge of the 55 girls studying in our Karnataka training center.

- For protection and God's blessing for our five sisters' teams as they go out for ministry.

- For God to use our 24 Karnataka student teams that will participate in a special summer outreach program.

May the Lord encourage you to trust Him as you follow His calling.

Your sister,

Gisela

20 Can You Be Trusted?

APRIL 2002

Dear Sister,

This morning I thought how nice it would be if I could visit you today. We could have a cup of coffee or tea together, and I could ask you how you are doing in your walk with the Lord, your family or Gospel team and in your ministry.

Of course, I don't know if you would feel free enough to share some of your difficulties and struggles with me.

Generally we all are very careful what we tell others, even as a prayer request, because we are afraid that the person we share it with may either judge us or spread the news around. It's so much safer to talk about our areas of strength than about the things with which we really need help or at least encouragement.

One of the saddest statements I hear from sisters who attend our Sisters' Seminars is: "Aunty, I can't share my problem with anyone. I don't dare talk about it with my family, my co-workers or the leadership, because someone surely will gossip."

I don't believe we should discuss every little difficulty we face in our homes or in the ministry with the rest of the world. Husbands and wives should especially do all they can to solve their differences before God and not expose each other's failures to the whole church. That in itself would easily turn into gossip.

I have been in worship services where, during testimony time, the wife stood up and asked for prayer for her husband, who was also a believer, and explained in detail how unkindly he treated her two days earlier. The poor husband sat in the men's section, publicly humiliated. That kind of exposure violates nearly everything God tells a wife about respecting and honoring her husband.

In one church my husband visited, the pastor took the right course of action. He stopped the wife's "prayer request" regarding her husband and asked her to sit down.

At the same time, God never intended for one of His children to be alone in his trials or without the counseling, prayers and ministry of the church. There are burdens, deep emotional pain, sickness and struggles that an individual is often unable to bear by himself or find biblical solutions for on his own. The clear teaching of the New Testament is that we all are members of one body, the Body of Christ. We are so closely knit together and interconnected that all that affects one member affects the whole body:

> And if one member suffers, all the members suffer with it;
> if one member is honored, all the members rejoice with it
> (1 Corinthians 12:26).

Furthermore, every member is called upon to supply the lack of the one that is in need of ministry:

Now we who are strong ought to bear the weaknesses of those without strength and not just please ourselves (Romans 15:1).

Bear one another's burdens, and thus fulfill the law of Christ (Galatians 6:2).

Therefore encourage one another, and build up one another (1 Thessalonians 5:11).

Is anyone among you sick? Let him call for the elders of the church, and let them pray over him, anointing him with oil in the name of the Lord (James 5:14).

Many brothers and sisters who need our ministry don't receive it because we can't be trusted! Gossip destroys our usefulness to God. If the believers in our church, our co-workers or the people of our mission field discover that we tell even one person what they shared with us confidentially, they will never trust us again. They will rather go without help or counseling than run the risk of being betrayed a second time.

The calling we have from the Lord is to represent Him and walk as He walked. Jesus surely never broke anyone's trust. Gossip is such a serious matter. We may be an excellent Bible teacher, a powerful witness and a great soul winner, but if we can't control our tongues, we destroy things faster than we can build them. Our tongues will ignite a forest fire that, before we know it, burns out of control.

Please study James 3:1–10 carefully and often. It will give you God's perspective on gossip. Let us not disqualify ourselves from serving others because we never learned to keep our mouths shut.

How confidentially should we treat confidential information? Because husband and wife are considered one before God, can they freely share confidential information with each other received during counseling—provided neither of them leaks it out?

In my opinion, the question is not whether or not the couple is able to keep the matter to themselves, but whether their action would violate in any way the trust and expectation of the person who poured out his heart. If we lose the trust of those who need our help, we can no longer minister to them.

I thought I would share with you how my husband and I deal with this matter of confidentiality. If someone talks to us as a couple about his problem and requests that we keep it confidential, my husband and I can talk and pray about it together, because it was entrusted to both of us. However, neither of us will pass the information on to anyone else.

If the person spoke to my husband alone, he will not share it with me, and I will not ask him to tell me. Likewise, if a sister shares her confidential problem with me, I will not mention it to my husband unless she specifically asks me to. If I feel that my husband could give her better advice or that it would be good for others to pray for the matter, I would first ask her permission. Sometimes a person may not tell me clearly whether the matter is to be treated as confidential or not. I always ask if I am not sure. That way I won't make a mistake. The only time I definitely would make an exception and pass on confidential information was if someone's life was in danger, such as if the person was planning to commit suicide or harm someone else.

I hope what I shared with you will be useful for your ministry.

I love you in Jesus,

Gisela

21 What Makes Your Faith Grow?

JUNE 2002

Dear Sister,

I am very thankful for your prayers for our family. It is God's grace alone that has protected us and kept us close to Himself until this day. All four of us are no different from the rest of God's children. We are not perfect, we don't have all the answers, we get discouraged and tired and we face the same uncertainties, struggles, trials and tests of our faith as you do. So all the things you pray for yourself, please pray them for us as well.

The importance of faith. Over these past few weeks, I have thought about the importance of faith in our walk with God. The Bible makes it very clear that everything in our Christian life must be the result of faith; otherwise, it will not please God and will be rejected by Him. *"And without faith it is impossible to please Him"* (Hebrews 11:6).

None of us is born without the ability to believe God if we choose to do so: *". . . as God has allotted to each a measure of faith"* (Romans 12:3). However, our initial measure of faith has the potential to grow; and God is extremely interested and desirous that it does, so He can fulfill His promises to us and we can bring glory to His name.

A statement the apostle Paul made about Abraham in Romans 4:20 caught my attention: *". . . he did not waver in unbelief, but grew strong in faith."* This verse tells me that Abraham's faith didn't start at "Level 10" where he could move mountains. It began small and grew in strength. Let us take a closer look at what caused Abraham's faith to grow and what it takes for our faith to grow as well.

As followers of Christ, we are called to a life of faith. It sounds exciting to trust God and to watch Him fulfill His promises in our lives, our families and our ministries. Abraham must have thought like this when God first called him to leave his country and relatives, go to a land He promised to give him as an inheritance and there become the father of many nations.

What Abraham didn't know was that his initial response to God's call wasn't enough to become a hero of faith overnight. In the same way we must not think that, after hearing a challenging message on faith or taking one successful step in believing God, we can easily live a life of faith.

God planned ahead. He knew from the very start that one day Abraham would have to face his greatest test of faith and obedience on Mount Moriah. There He would ask him to sacrifice Isaac, the son God had promised and given him through a miracle.

Abraham would not know that the sacrifice was just a test or of the merciful outcome God had planned. The only way Abraham could pass this ultimate test would be if he had learned ahead of time how to cling by faith to God's promises.

With this in mind, God set out to practically train Abraham in believing in His Word when surrounded by impossibilities.

Faith grows not by theory but by practice. Over the next few decades, God gave Abraham many opportunities to practice faith. Each time, he learned more about God's character and His faithfulness to keep His Word. We can clearly see that Abraham's faith grew, not by just talking about it, but by exercising it.

On several occasions Abraham started out in faith but then lacked the endurance to believe until he saw God's promise come to pass. Other times he acted out of fear instead of faith or employed his own wisdom. Each time God patiently corrected him and let him continue practicing faith until he could pass the test he had failed earlier.

Do you know how Abraham developed endurance in trusting God? The answer is in James 1:3: *". . . the testing of your faith produces endurance."* That endurance, which he acquired through many tests, was the key that enabled him to trust God on Mount Moriah when nothing the Lord asked him to do seemed to make sense.

Look at what Abraham was able to believe God for: *"By faith Abraham, when he was tested, offered up Isaac. . . . It was he to whom it was said, 'In Isaac your seed shall be called.' He considered that God is able to raise men even from the dead"* (Hebrews 11:17–19).

When we study Abraham's life, we find that each time he succeeded in trusting God, a more difficult situation arose, designed to stretch his faith even further. All the difficulties, hardships and impossibilities Abraham encountered actually became stepping-stones of faith and opportunities to grow in his trust in God and bring glory to Him.

Please know that God has never changed His training method since Abraham. For our faith to grow in strength, God must give us opportunities to practice faith and tests to help us learn endurance.

What motivates us to exercise faith? Have you ever noticed, in your own life, that faith is usually the very last thing we consider, only after we run out of all other ideas and resources in trying to solve a problem? God knows well that we see little need for exercising faith unless we encounter a situation that is beyond any solution we can find. I am almost certain that if Abraham had a choice, he would have picked out an easier way to become the father of faith, rather than going from one desperate situation to another.

Our heavenly Father desires so much to fulfill in our lives all He has promised in His Word, but He can't unless we exercise faith. Have you ever considered that it could be God's amazing love that permits needs and impossible circumstances in our lives so we have no other option left than to cling to Him in faith? And each time we do, we experience His faithfulness to His Word, and as a result, our faith grows.

Dear Sister, there is not one difficult situation we encounter in our life that doesn't have the potential of becoming a stepping-stone of faith. I hope that this will encourage you as God gives you opportunities to exercise faith, so you can grow in strength and endurance like Abraham did.

Please pray with us for:

- All the new students who are joining our Bible schools this month.

- The opening of our primary schools.

With love and prayers,

Gisela

22 Becoming an Example

Dear Sister,

It's now been several weeks since I returned home from traveling to Germany, India and Sri Lanka.

Our children, Daniel and Sarah, came home for a few weeks during their summer break. I traveled back with them to India, and we stopped in Germany to visit my mother. She was so happy to see her grandchildren and me as well. My mother will be 88 years old next month. Her health is still quite good, and she is able to take care of herself. In fact, she is usually busy all day, working in and around her house. We helped her plant flowers and vegetables in her garden, which is her favorite place to be. I would appreciate it if you would remember her in your prayers.

A few days after we reached India, the first Sisters' Seminar on my trip took place in Tripura. I was very happy to go there—it was the first northeast Indian state I was able to visit, because much of the region experienced years of struggles and violence. For this reason, my coming was unannounced, and many of our GFA families committed themselves to pray specifically for this meeting and my travels. I stayed at our training center and had the privilege to get to know Brother Anil, our Tripura leader, his wife, Suchitra, their sweet children and our GFA staff. I am so thankful for their vision and burden to reach the people of Tripura with the love of God and for their faithfulness in the midst of many struggles.

Our GFA training center began in 1996 with 60 students and was the very first Bible school in the state of Tripura. Since then, our graduates and students have established more than 200 churches and fellowships. It's truly God's grace—and a very ripe harvest field. While I was there, I had the joy of attending a baptism service for several new believers. It was held at a nearby fishpond where, since 1996, more than 500 people have confessed Christ publicly.

Our Sisters' Seminar went well. More than 200 sisters attended, and I especially liked their singing. Together we studied what God's Word says about Christian marriage, family life and serving the Lord as a woman. During the final session, many of the sisters came forward to share what God showed them during the sessions and what they were planning to apply in their lives. It was such a blessing to see their sincerity and love for the Lord.

Though I could only be there for a few days, I felt the Lord was going to answer my prayers and allow me to have a small part in the salvation of Tripura through encouraging my sisters.

Our next two seminars took place in Orissa, India, and Sri

Lanka. Perhaps I will share a little about these two places in my next letter.

On the majority of our mission fields, the brothers and sisters who came to Christ are first-generation Christians. That's exciting and truly an answer to prayer. In addition, a large number of our missionaries are also from a non-Christian background. This means that in many places, everyone in the church, including the pastor and his wife, grew up in families and communities where people's behavior and lifestyle were not based on biblical values.

Often there are no older, more mature Christians in the churches the new believers can learn from because the fellowships have been only recently established. Naturally the new believers will look to their pastor and his family to show them what it means to live for Jesus and have a Christian marriage and family life.

Perhaps you assumed it was mainly the pastor's job to be the model for everyone in the church. However, a large portion of every congregation will be made up of young girls and women. The pastor can only teach them what the Bible says about their roles as sisters, wives and mothers. The practical demonstration of how to live these roles needs to come from sisters who know the Lord and follow this biblical teaching.

I can assure you, whether you are leading a sisters' Gospel team or you are the wife of a leader, pastor or Bible schoolteacher, all the sisters in your team, church or Bible school will closely observe you. Whatever you do in the church, at home or in the community, the other sisters will copy you. The reason is that you may be the only Christian woman who has known the Lord longer than they have. Perhaps they feel because you had some Bible training or you are married to a pastor, you surely must live what the Bible says, and so they will desire to become like you.

It's a huge responsibility to be an example for others, but that's part of our calling as servants of God.

The real problem arises if what we practice in our own life doesn't line up with the Word of God and then others copy our actions, thinking that what they learn from us is normal Christian behavior. Before long, the people who imitate us will exhibit our weaknesses in their character, which will greatly diminish the testimony and effectiveness of the church.

What should you do to become an example others can follow?

1. Seek to know God through spending time with Him and His Word. Worship Him and love Him above everything else in this world. His presence will become your greatest treasure: *"I count all things to be loss in view of the surpassing value of knowing Christ Jesus my Lord"* (Philippians 3:8).

2. Let the Word of God continuously correct your thinking, values and behavior: *"All Scripture is inspired by God and profitable for teaching, for reproof, for correction, for training in righteousness"* (2 Timothy 3:16). Compare what you practice in every area of your life, including your marriage and family life, with what the Bible teaches on the subject. Each time you discover a difference between the two, change according to the Word of God. Obedience is the key to a genuine Christian walk.

3. Live with the awareness that others are watching and learning from you. Don't be careless in your behavior or in the words you speak. Remember what the apostle Paul says in 2 Corinthians 3:2–3: *"You are our letter . . . known and read by all men; being manifested that you are a letter of Christ."*

I invite you to intercede with us for our GFA ministry in Tripura:

- For a peaceful solution to the conflict between the Bengalis and the tribal communities.

- For protection of all our Tripura missionaries, students, churches and the Bible school.

- For much fruit from our radio broadcast in the Kok Borok language.

- For a church in every village.

I pray for you, that you will serve Jesus with great joy and all your heart.

Your sister,

Gisela

23 How God Equips You to Serve

OCTOBER 2002

Dear Sister,

A few weeks ago, Mike and Jane from our GFA office in the USA had their first baby, Benjamin.

We are all so happy and praise God together with them, because they waited for this child for nearly 20 years. All these many years, they were clinging by faith to God's promise that He would give them a child. They even had a room with a baby bed ready and prepared for the day when God would answer their prayers.

In the meantime, they both served God full-time and with great faithfulness and joy. In fact, Jane filled our office with laughter and singing like no one else. I am certain Mike and Jane had their times of struggles and discouragement. But instead of living a life of sadness, despair and frustration, they considered these past 20 years as a special time God gave them to serve Him with undivided attention and all their strength.

When we look at Mike and Jane's journey of faith as a couple, there is so much we can learn from them for our own walks with the Lord. In this letter, I would like to explain a little why God leads us through times of waiting for answers to our prayers, testing of our faith and struggles from within and around us.

It's for our personal growth as Christians. If God would fulfill our prayers and expectations and give us a smooth life without any adversities, we would forever remain weak, immature Christians. As much as physical exercise is vital for a small child to learn how to sit, stand and walk, we as believers need spiritual exercise to develop in our Christian lives.

The more we are forced by circumstances to learn to trust God and overcome adversities, the more our faith grows and the more Christlike we become.

Please read the story of Joseph beginning in Genesis 37, and count how many struggles he faced. He was misunderstood and hated by his brothers, thrown in a well, sold as a slave to Egypt, separated from his family, lived as a Hebrew among idol worshipers, falsely accused, imprisoned for many years and forgotten by the royal official who could have helped him get out.

The Bible lists only the big struggles, but I am very certain there were hundreds of smaller ones Joseph faced daily in his heart: discouragement, sadness, feeling homesick and lonely . . . wondering if his father, mother and brothers were still alive and if they ever found out the real reason for his disappearance . . . dealing with anger over what happened to him . . . feeling helpless as a slave with no rights . . . suffering daily humiliation . . . being taken advantage of and treated as a piece of property . . . worrying about his future . . . battling the temptation to compromise his faith and convictions . . . wondering why God had not rescued him, answered his prayers or fulfilled the dreams.

God used each of these obstacles in Joseph's life to help him grow not only in his faith, endurance and ability to cling to God, but also in his character. Joseph became a man of integrity, faithfulness, forgiveness, obedience and patience. He learned courage to stand alone, serving and caring for others—instead of wallowing in self-pity—and waiting for God's timing.

It's also for equipping us to serve others who face similar circumstances. The apostle Paul wrote in 2 Corinthians 1:3–7:

> . . . the Father of mercies and God of all comfort; who comforts us in all our affliction so that we may be able to comfort those who are in any affliction with the same comfort with which we ourselves are comforted by God. For just as the sufferings of Christ are ours in abundance, so also our comfort is abundant through Christ. But if we are afflicted, it is for your comfort and salvation; or if we are comforted, it is for your comfort, which is effective in the patient enduring of the same sufferings which we also suffer; and our hope for you is firmly grounded, knowing that as you are sharers of our sufferings, so also you are sharers of our comfort.

This Scripture says that God doesn't leave His children alone in their struggles. He has already prepared someone who faced a similar trial to understand, encourage, comfort and strengthen us.

None of us will go through every adversity there is on this planet, but each of us will go through some. And in all those we experienced and overcame by the grace of God, we become qualified to serve and strengthen others.

If you were in prison, Joseph would be the perfect person to visit, encourage and comfort you. If you were beaten and stoned, you would get the most understanding from the apostle Paul or a GFA missionary who experienced such an attack. And if you and your husband had been praying for many years for a child, Mike and Jane would be able to encourage you the most.

Even if you find no one else who faces the struggles you go through, you will always have Jesus. He faced all our temptations (Hebrews 4:15), and He bore all our sorrows and afflictions at the cross (Isaiah 53:4–6). His comfort is perfect and His grace sufficient in our weakness (2 Corinthians 12:9).

As believers, our ministry to the Body of Christ expands with every victory we win in our battles. Though trials, testing, struggles and adversities are things we would rather avoid—and often complain about—they are the very things that cause us to grow, overcome and become useful in serving God.

I hope this letter will encourage you in following Jesus.

Let us join our hearts and pray in faith for the release of Brother Manja from prison in Nepal (our brother was falsely accused and received a 20-year sentence):

• For God to sustain his health and spiritual strength.

• For all those who come in contact with him to receive Christ as a result.

- For comfort and strength for his dear wife and children.

- For his church to become a powerful witness for the whole country of Nepal.

May you walk in the grace of God always.

Your sister,

Gisela

24 God's Amazing Love

DECEMBER 2002

Dear Sister,

Before I started writing this letter to you, I opened my Bible and read the Christmas story in Luke 2.

Christmas is my favorite time of the year, and I look forward to our family being at home for the holidays. At the end of November, I will visit my mother in Germany and then travel back home. My husband, along with Daniel and Sarah, will arrive from India a week later. This year we will spend Christmas and New Year's with our staff in the United States.

Each time we celebrate the birth of Jesus our Savior, we are reminded afresh of the amazing love God has for this lost world and for each one of us. I would like to encourage you to take time this Christmas to learn more about God's love, which is the very reason for our salvation.

The Bible tells us that the living God not only loves us, but that He *is* love. *"And we have come to know and have believed the love which God has for us. God is love . . ."* (1 John 4:16). This means God is not only capable of showing love, but His very nature *is* love.

Let me explain. A bird, for example, grows feathers, flies through the air, builds a nest, lays eggs and eats seeds. Why does he do all these things? He does it because he has a bird-nature, and these things are normal and consistent with what he is.

God's nature is love, and consequently, everything He does is consistent with who He is. That means every word He speaks and every one of His actions originate from and are governed by His love-nature. If we understand and believe this, we will be able to trust Him without fear. Even when He corrects us or allows us to go through difficult circumstances, we will always be secure in His love.

God's love toward us will never change because His nature is unchanging: *"For I, the LORD, do not change"* (Malachi 3:6).

The level of friendship and human love people extend to each other is for the most part based on performance or temporary affection. If circumstances change or we act contrary to others' expectations, they are disappointed and their love and interest in us diminish or cease altogether. We often fear to lose the love of those around us after saying or doing something they don't like or when we fail an exam, don't get the job we applied for or earn the money they expected.

Likewise, many believers assume God's love toward them depends on their flawless performance as Christians. Each time they fall short, they feel God is disappointed with them and therefore loves them less. In order to earn His love back, they try to work harder on being good enough to deserve it. I have known parents who tell a child, "If you are not nice to your brother or don't do your homework, God doesn't love you. He only loves good children." Nothing could be further from the truth! Our performances, failures or successes do not influence His love toward us. Neither does anything else we may encounter. His love remains the same for all eternity, because God Himself never changes.

The apostle Paul wrote about this subject:

> *For I am convinced that neither death, nor life, nor angels, nor principalities, nor things present, nor things to come, nor powers, nor height, nor depth, nor any other created thing, shall be able to separate us from the love of God, which is in Christ Jesus our Lord* (Romans 8:38–39).

We get to know the heart of our heavenly Father when we study what the Bible tells us about divine love:

> *Love is patient, love is kind, and is not jealous; love does not brag and is not arrogant, does not act unbecomingly; it does not seek its own, is not provoked, does not take into account a wrong suffered, does not rejoice in unrighteousness, but rejoices with the truth; bears all things, believes all things, hopes all things, endures all things. Love never fails* (1 Corinthians 13:4–8).

Because God is love, these verses are actually a detailed description of Himself. I encourage you to read them once more by exchanging the word "love" with "my heavenly Father" or "Jesus." The more we know our God, the more we will enjoy His presence, because *"there is no fear in love"* (1 John 4:18). We truly are the most privileged people on the face of the earth.

Did you know that when you became a child of God you received His love-nature?

> *... in order that by them [His promises] you might become partakers of the divine nature* (2 Peter 1:4).

> *The love of God has been poured out within our hearts through the Holy Spirit who was given to us* (Romans 5:5).

God's wonderful and amazing love has been given to us because we became part of His family. And that love sets us apart from the rest of this world and is our mark of recognition as Christians: *"By this all men will know that you are My disciples, if you have love for one another"* (John 13:35).

I believe the Lord wants us to use the love He has given us to share the Good News with all those who need a Savior—this Christmas and throughout the coming year.

Please pray with us as we look forward to the year 2003:

- That God may grant us peace on all the mission fields.

- For many new open doors to preach the Gospel.

- That all our missionaries and their families will be faithful to Christ and to the calling God has placed on their lives.

My dear Sister, I wish you God's wonderful peace and His joy as you celebrate Christmas and enter a new year of service to the King of kings.

With love and prayers,

Gisela

25 Replacing Fear with Faith

FEBRUARY 2003

Dear Sister,

May God's grace and peace be with you every day of this new year. As I write to you, my children and my husband have just left for India. It's so quiet in my house, and I miss them a lot. In a few weeks I will also be traveling. In the meantime, I hope to finish a few writing projects.

In this letter I hope to share something important with you that will bring stability to your Christian life—if you practice it.

Each time we enter a new year, we are confronted with 365 unknown days that tend to fill our hearts with fear. Our fear is based on what we experienced in the past, the things we see happening around us and our thoughts that usually imagine the worst.

For example, if our children were seriously sick last summer, we anxiously wait to see if it will happen again this year. If opposition to the Christian faith is increasing around us, we worry that we might have to quit our church-planting work and move somewhere else. If someone we love bitterly disappointed us or betrayed our trust, we are afraid it will happen again.

If we start thinking about the possibilities of political turmoil, travel accidents, persecution, martyrdom, lack of money to live on, our children failing their school exams, family problems, difficulties in our marriage, failing health, disunity in the church, power struggles among co-workers—and a thousand other terrible things—we will not have a single peaceful day in 2003.

In the face of all these real-life threats, the Bible tells us:

> *Rejoice in the Lord always; again I will say, rejoice!* (Philippians 4:4)

> *Be anxious for nothing, but in everything by prayer and supplication with thanksgiving let your requests be made known to God* (Philippians 4:6).

> *Rejoice always; pray without ceasing; in everything give thanks; for this is God's will for you in Christ Jesus* (1 Thessalonians 5:16–18).

Are we to close our eyes to reality? The truth is, the world we live in is not getting better. We are surrounded by wars, terrorism, persecution, sickness and all those things I listed above. As Christians, we are not immune to life's struggles as long as we live in this fallen world. In addition, Satan is our enemy, and we are constantly engaged in a spiritual battle.

God doesn't ask us to close our eyes to reality or pretend that nothing negative can ever happen to us.

Instead, God wants us to change our focus from the fearful things of this earth to Him. Only when I look at my heavenly Father can I put all the threatening things that surround me in this world in the right perspective. It then will become real to me that:

- My heavenly Father loves me: *". . . for the Father Himself loves you"* (John 16:27).

- He knows every one of my needs: *". . . for your heavenly Father knows that you need all these things"* (Matthew 6:32).

- He cares for me: *". . . casting all your anxiety upon Him, because He cares for you"* (1 Peter 5:7).

- He bears my burden: *"Blessed be the Lord, who daily bears our burden"* (Psalm 68:19).

- He doesn't want me to worry: *"Be anxious for nothing"* (Philippians 4:6).

- He invites me to tell Him all my concerns: *". . . in everything by prayer and supplication with thanksgiving let your requests be made known to God"* (Philippians 4:6).

- He is all-powerful: *"For nothing will be impossible with God"* (Luke 1:37).

- He is well able to rescue me from whatever I face: *". . . our God whom we serve is able to deliver us"* (Daniel 3:17).

- If He chooses for me to go through trials, He is with me and brings me safely through: *"Even though I walk through the valley of the shadow of death, I fear no evil; for Thou art with me"* (Psalm 23:4).

- There is nothing He would not do for me: *"He who did not spare His own Son, but delivered Him up for us all, how will He not also with Him freely give us all things?"* (Romans 8:32).

Learning to focus on my heavenly Father will replace my fear with faith. Faith will enable me to rejoice and give thanks, like the apostle Paul wrote in 1 Thessalonians 5:16–18, because I trust Him to have a solution for me.

It will give me peace in the midst of a storm, because I know He can handle my situation.

It assures me that He knows all the unknowns of my life and that I am safe in His arms.

Faith is what pleases God and what moves His hand to work on my behalf (Hebrews 11:6; Matthew 21:22).

Faith is the shield with which I must protect myself during an attack from Satan. With it I will be able to extinguish *all* the flaming missiles of the enemy (Ephesians 6:16).

During this year of 2003, I challenge you to practice replacing your fear with faith. Each time your circumstances or imagination fills you with fear, stop entertaining your fearful thoughts. Instead, meditate on each of the Bible verses I listed about focusing on our heavenly Father.

As you do, look at your situation or fear in the light of each verse, and ask God to make His Word alive to you. If going through these Scriptures once is not enough to replace your fear with faith, do it 5, 10 or 20 times—until your spirit is able to believe God's Word. If the same fear attacks you two days, three weeks or five years later, go through the Scriptures again.

This is what I do when I am afraid or when faced with problems. The Scriptures I cling to may vary with different situations, but the end result *must* be faith; otherwise, there will be no victory.

After you have learned how to replace fear with faith, teach it to others so that they too will become strong in the Lord our God.

Let's pray for one another and for the thousands of believers in our churches, that God will help us become a people of faith with whom He can change this world.

With love and
prayer,

Gisela

26 Finding Fulfillment in Obedience

APRIL 2003

Dear Sister,

In your service to the Lord, I am sure your life has to be flexible. Mine does too!

One evening in February, I got a call from my husband that I should leave for India the next day at noon to attend an important meeting. It was quite a challenge to get ready with such short notice. But I made it to the airport in time, and I reached my destination the evening before the meeting took place. It was good to see Daniel and Sarah as well. Now I am back home, and I am busy with the work for our ministry.

This morning I was thinking about our Bible school students and the challenges they are faced with right after graduation. In this letter I want to write something that should help them—and all of us—to make the right decisions as we seek to follow the Lord.

How much courage do we have when God asks us to do something we have never done before or something we think we have no talent to accomplish? Perhaps it would be more accurate to ask ourselves this: How much willingness do we have to obey Him and step out in faith?

When I look back at my own life, as a young Christian I was eager to serve the Lord in evangelism and outreach ministry. I enjoyed being on the front lines, and I imagined that after my marriage this would be the main area where I would help my husband in his ministry. However, to my surprise, God began to ask me to do things I never wanted to do—or thought I couldn't do.

While I was growing up, my mother worked in a bank. Seeing her sitting at an office desk every day and doing paperwork, I decided that this would be the one thing I would never do in my life. I was willing to serve the Lord at the end of the world . . . but not sitting at a desk.

Guess what the Lord had planned for me? He began giving me things to do such as mailing prayer letters, replying to people's questions regarding our ministry, sending thank you notes to prayer partners and eventually writing a few small stories for a devotional booklet. Later on, when we had no writer for our monthly prayer letters and reports, writing became my regular job. Today, years later, I am involved in writing for all sorts of our ministry publications, including several books.

Was it easy for me to switch from wanting to do outreach ministry to sitting at a desk and writing? Perhaps not at first. But I discovered that my fulfillment and joy in serving the Lord did not come from getting to do what I imagined, but from obedience to the Lord's will. I can honestly say I do my writing with the same heart commitment as I would do outreach work.

There were a lot of things I needed to learn on the job. I didn't have writers' training, and English is not my mother tongue. It stretched and challenged my faith to believe God that He would give me the ability to do new writing projects I had never done before. I also learned to humbly accept correction from others. I remember well, in the beginning, how my husband would read what I composed and cross half out, asking me to rewrite it. This would happen several times until it sounded right.

The Lord was faithful to give me a dear friend, Heidi, who is a writer for our ministry as well. She edits my work before it goes for publication. That way my English grammar and expressions are correct. We have worked together for many years; some of you met her when she traveled with me to several of our Sisters' Seminars more than a year ago.

Why am I telling you all these stories? I suspect that one of these days, the Lord may want to teach you some of the same lessons He wanted me to learn.

Let me encourage you *not* to choose the easy road and refuse to do something new or something you wouldn't plan for yourself. This is your opportunity to step out in faith and learn to trust Him. I promise you will be amazed at the wonderful things God will do through your life if you allow Him to lead you beyond your comfort zone.

If you feel unqualified or afraid, you are not alone. The Bible is full of people who felt just the same.

Please read the story of Moses' calling in Exodus 3 and 4. God was ready to deliver the Israelites out of slavery. He assigned the task to a man who did his best to convince the Lord that he couldn't do it. These were Moses' arguments:

I am a nobody (3:11), I don't know what to say (3:13), I am sure no one will believe me or listen to me (4:1), I can't speak well (4:10) and I don't want to be the messenger (4:13).

Do any of these reasons sound familiar to you? Have you tried to convince yourself, and God, with similar ones? God had news for Moses. He didn't want his abilities and talents—all He looked for was his willingness and obedience. God was going to take care of the rest. He told Moses:

I will be with you (3:12), I will do the miracles (3:20), I will teach you what to say (4:12), I will give you an assistant (4:14), I will be with your mouth and his mouth (4:15) and I will teach you what you are to do (4:15).

Imagine for a moment that Moses refused God's call and stayed with his sheep in the wilderness. He would never have known what the Lord could accomplish through his life—simply by putting his faith in God when offered a job he thought he couldn't do.

My dear Sister, the same promises God gave to Moses are for you as well. I pray that when God asks you to step out in faith, you will do it. The God who parted the Red Sea when Moses was willing to trust Him will do whatever it takes for you to accomplish His will.

Let us pray together for:

- God's anointing upon our Bible school graduates who have just entered full-time ministry.

- His protection and empowerment for thousands of our students on summer outreach.

- Many new churches to be planted as a result.

I hope that what I've shared with you will encourage you in your walk with the Lord.

Your sister,

Gisela

27 Breaking the Captivity of Your Past

June 2003

Dear Sister,

My life became so much more exciting when at the end of April my husband, along with Daniel and Sarah, came home from India. Our children were here for a month. During this time, they helped in our GFA office, attended our staff retreat and did things for us at home. Sarah planted flowers and rosebushes in our yard, which I now enjoy every day.

In my letter I want to address how we can live for Jesus, free from the influence of negative experiences we have faced in our lives.

We are held captive by our past. None of us was brought up in a perfect family or society. Since the fall of man, such an environment no longer exists on earth. We all carry scars from being misunderstood, disappointed, lonely, rejected or treated unfairly at some point in our lives. Perhaps we grew up in poverty and had to miss out on many things and opportunities others enjoyed, or we experienced deep hurt and unhappiness because of family problems, neglect or sickness.

Whatever it may be we went through, it left a permanent mark on our lives. In fact, the way we think about the world around us, how we deal with people and how we interpret words and actions have much to do with our past experiences. For example, if a child grew up in a situation where he was often lied to or taken advantage of, as an adult he will have a hard time trusting anyone.

Some of these scars hinder us from living the kind of life we long for, but we don't know how to free ourselves from their control. Is it possible for us as Christians to escape the influence and captivity of our past experiences—or will they haunt us for the rest of our lives?

The Bible states that when we received Christ, we became a new creation. *"Therefore if any man is in Christ, he is a new creature; the old things passed away; behold, new things have come"* (2 Corinthians 5:17).

Each one of us can testify to the changes that immediately took place when we received Jesus as our Savior and Lord: Our sins were forgiven, we were delivered from Satan's power, we found peace with God, we became sons and daughters of God, our names were written down in the Book of Life and we were on our way to heaven.

We also noticed that when we acted contrary to our new nature, our heart became troubled, whereas before we couldn't care less. That's because now the Holy Spirit lives inside of us. He teaches us right from wrong and helps us learn to live and act in accordance with our new nature.

However, this new nature resides in our old bodies and must live through our mind and emotions, which are scarred by past experiences. They will indeed greatly hinder God's life from flowing freely through us if they continue to act based on our negative past.

God knows this. That's why He wants our mind to be completely renewed (Romans 12:2), which happens through the Word of God.

This sets in motion a transformation of our entire being, which is God's ultimate goal for every believer: *"to become conformed to the image of His Son"* (Romans 8:29). Being like Jesus will leave absolutely no room for old scars to survive and dominate our walk with God.

The devil told us a lie! Many believers—even after knowing the Lord for a long time—still blame the disappointments and bitter experiences of their past for their inability to trust and love others, take responsibility for their actions, become transparent with other believers, submit to authority or live in victory.

Why is it that they can't seem to rise above their scars? Because they believe a lie of the devil, who has told them that they can't escape their past, however hard they may try. That lie has prevented them from surrendering their problem area to the Holy Spirit and experiencing His healing power, deliverance and transformation.

As believers, we have a choice to either believe the devil or God's Word, which says:

> . . . *the old things passed away; behold, new things have come* (2 Corinthians 5:17).

If therefore the Son shall make you free, you shall be free indeed (John 8:36).

Now may the God of peace Himself sanctify you entirely; and may your spirit and soul and body be preserved complete, without blame at the coming of our Lord Jesus Christ. Faithful is He who calls you, and He also will bring it to pass (1 Thessalonians 5:23–24).

As we put our faith in God's promises, He will touch our lives, heal our scars and transform us into the likeness of Christ. But first we must *want* to change with all our heart. This means we must give up shedding tears, feeling sorry for ourselves or blaming circumstances. Instead, each time our scars bother us, we must deliberately choose to act on God's Word. We will be surprised at the freedom that comes as a result.

It worked for me! As a young believer, one of the things I struggled with was my inability to open myself to others. Early in my life, I had closed my heart to others and wouldn't allow them to know me. My salvation and God's call brought many changes in my life, but not in this area.

About five years later, I learned about the transforming power of the Holy Spirit, and I asked Him to fill my life. He did, and shortly afterward, God made it clear to me that He couldn't use me for others unless I opened up my life. I obeyed in faith because I loved Him, and in response the Holy Spirit began to transform that area of my life. Today I could never share God's Word—and my life—with you and the thousands of other sisters if this hadn't happened. I praise God for His faithfulness.

Dear Sister, what God did for me, He will also do for you! Give Him your scars—and experience His power to change you.

Let's pray together and ask God to bless:

- The two new radio broadcasts in Tibetan languages that started in March.

- Preparation for 15 additional radio programs that will be added this year.

- All the new Bible school students who start their classes this month.

May you experience the love and grace of God in your daily walk with Him.

In Jesus,

Gisela

28 Did the Changes Last?

AUGUST 2003

Dear Sister,

It's rainy season in Kerala, India. I arrived here at our ABS campus a few days ago after spending a week in North India. Right now I am sitting on my bed writing this letter to you. A few minutes ago the electricity went off, and now I am looking at the sky to see when the rain will start up again. Last night it was pouring hard. We had the windows open, and I could hear the frogs croaking all night long. They must be asleep now, since it's daytime; only the crickets are making chirping noises.

My husband is here as well. All our senior leaders have come from every part of India and the neighboring countries for a leaders meeting. They are seeking the Lord's mind and working hard for the future development of Believers Church.

When I see these brothers the Lord has called to lead and oversee our church movement and ministries, I am so thankful. Each one is deeply committed to the Lord and has a burden for the church and a passion to reach the unreached. How blessed we are to have such godly leaders.

Please remember to faithfully pray for them. Their responsibilities are many. They need the Lord's encouragement and wisdom, as well as His protection for their many travels. And please don't forget to equally pray for their wives and children. They must make many sacrifices so their husbands and fathers are free to serve the Lord.

From June 23–25 we had a Family Conference in Ambala, Haryana. Brother Simon, our leader for the northern states of India, his wife, Mini, and their children all traveled with me by train from Delhi to Ambala. We had a wonderful time of fellowship. I always look forward to spending time with this dear family.

About 170 delegates from the states of Himachal Pradesh and Haryana took part in the meeting. The teaching centered around Christian marriage, family life, raising children, being a pastor's family and serving the Lord together as a couple. The content of the teaching was very similar to the many sisters' meetings we have held over the past few years. However, for the first time, 40 of our pastors and their wives attended the meeting together.

This turned out to be very helpful to these couples, because they could hear the same teaching and later discuss it in our feedback sessions. Many of them made decisions about how to implement what they had learned in their family life and ministry. Our leaders believe that such family conferences will strengthen our pastors' families and our churches. They are hoping to conduct more in the days to come.

Did you have an opportunity to attend one of our Sisters' Seminars or Family Conferences over the past few years? If you did, I am curious to know if what you learned helped you. I know that many sisters made decisions during the meetings, but I wonder what actually took place when you returned home or rejoined your Gospel team or Bible school.

If you are married, I would like to know what *specific* changes took place in your relationship with your husband, in your family life and in your ministry. Did your husband notice any positive changes in you, and did these changes last? What *specifically* would you want to learn more about?

If you are unmarried, I would like to know if anything *specific* changed in your personal life, walk with the Lord and ministry. Did your relationship to your team members or fellow Bible school students improve? Did your leaders and teachers notice any positive changes in you, and did these changes last? What *specifically* would you want to learn more about?

I would appreciate if you could write me a note and mail it to your regional office. They will be kind to translate and forward it to me. Your response will help us improve our future family conferences, and we will make sure to include those things that are the most helpful to the delegates.

In addition, I am in the process of putting into book format all the subjects we studied in our Sisters' Seminars and Family Conferences. It is about two-thirds finished. Your feedback at this time would be valuable to me. I also would very much appreciate your prayers so that the Lord will enable me to complete the book soon. Then I will have more time to travel to our mission fields.

Dear Sister, before I close this letter, I want to encourage you to serve the Lord with all your heart. He will come back soon, and when we see Him, all our struggles and problems will seem insignificant in the light of His glory. He is truly worthy of giving our all in serving Him.

I invite you to join us in prayer for the country of Bangladesh.

- Pray for our leader Brother Kiran and his family. They lost a number of relatives in a landslide during the recent cyclone.

- Our second Bible school was destroyed as well. None of the 40 students was killed. However, we now need a new building for their Bible school training.

- Pray that the Lord may meet the needs of our churches, believers and all those who were affected by the cyclone.

- Pray that the Lord may use our brothers and sisters in Bangladesh to win their country for Jesus.

May God's love and grace be with you always.

Your sister,

Gisela

29 Holiness Is What We Need

OCTOBER 2003

Dear Sister,

During the month of August, my husband and I attended a missions conference in England. One of the speakers made a statement that spoke to my heart. He said:

The greatest need of my people is my greater holiness. And the greatest need of your people is your greater holiness.

He was right! How often do we think thoughts like these: "If only the people in our church were more committed, our fellowship would grow faster ... If only our team members had more boldness in evangelism, our outreach would be more fruitful ... If only my family members had more faith, God could do miracles and meet our needs ... If only my husband would treat me with more understanding, my home life would be happier ..."

Even if we don't say it, most of the time we believe the reason why God can't move or bless as He promised in His Word is because the fault lies with others. We are blind to our own need for greater holiness, brokenness and humility. That's why we pray for God to change those around us when all the while, God longs to change us.

What is holiness? The meaning of holiness is described in the dictionary with words such as piety, sanctity, godliness, saintliness, consecration (being set apart), devoutness, devotion and purity.

It's difficult for us to imagine how holiness looks in someone's life until we realize it's the very nature and character of our God: *"I the LORD your God am holy"* (Leviticus 19:2).

This, and many other Scriptures, tells us God is holy. If we want to know what holiness is, all we need to do is observe our God. This became possible when Jesus took on human form and walked on this earth. He lived and served God in complete holiness. This means He was wholly set apart and devoted to His Father in heaven, seeking only to do His will. That's why He did not spare Himself but was obedient unto death on the cross.

There was no impurity, such as pride, pretense or seeking honor, in His motives, thoughts, words and actions. Neither was there any selfish ambition in His ministry nor a double standard in His private and public life.

Looking at Jesus, we come to the conclusion that holiness is living and serving God with no mixture of self-life.

To be holy is to be Christlike. That's what God desires for us to become:

Like the Holy One who called you, be holy yourselves also in all your behavior; because it is written, "YOU SHALL BE HOLY, FOR I AM HOLY" (1 Peter 1:15–16).

He chose us in Him before the foundation of the world, that we should be holy and blameless before Him (Ephesians 1:4).

What helps us become more holy?

1. Accepting God's correction and discipline in all those areas not wholly given to Him: *". . . but He disciplines us for our good, that we may share His holiness"* (Hebrews 12:10).

2. Our own commitment to separation and cleansing from those things that promote self-life, such as setting our affection on the things of this world, an unwillingness to submit and seeking our own interests instead of God's will. *"Let us cleanse ourselves from all defilement of flesh and spirit, perfecting holiness in the fear of God"* (2 Corinthians 7:1).

What effect has our greater holiness on our ministry and others?

The holier, and therefore more pure, our walk with God becomes, the brighter the light of the Gospel shines through us—without us trying to make it happen. People will automatically encounter Jesus when they meet us. Our message will be clearer and less hindered by our self-life, drawing people to Jesus.

God will have to spend less time dealing with our selfish motives and setting our hearts right before He can use us. We will be available to serve Him whenever He chooses.

When other believers come in contact with us, they will recognize their own need to grow and change. That's what happened when people met Jesus.

Dear Sister, because God desires holiness for our lives, let us long for it as well and yield to Him when He works on us to bring it about.

Please pray with us for our radio ministry. This month we are adding 15 new languages. This brings our total to 69 broadcasts. Please pray:

- For God's anointing for all our broadcasters, that they will proclaim the Gospel with power.

- For clear reception in each listening area.

- For much response, especially from the new languages.

May you experience God's love and closeness each day.

Your sister in Christ,

Gisela

30 Your Reason to Rejoice

Dear Sister,

How fast the year has gone by! It's December and this is my last letter to you in 2003.

My plans for the second half of this year changed in a way I hadn't imagined. After visiting England and speaking at our Family Conference in North India in August, I went to Kerala to be with my husband and our children for a week. On the 9th of September, I left for Germany to visit my mother for her 89th birthday. The day before I was to leave for the USA, my mother became seriously sick. She was admitted to the hospital to undergo an operation. I canceled my flight and stayed in the hospital with her and afterward at her house. Finally I was able to return home on the 19th of October.

The extra weeks I was gone left my husband and me with only a little time at home together, and it also delayed much of my writing schedule. Yet God gave me peace to trust Him regarding this change of plans. I would greatly appreciate it if you would remember my mother in your prayers and believe the Lord together with us to heal her completely. Thank you!

I wonder how things have gone with you over the past 12 months.

Thank God for His blessings. Surely the Lord has blessed you in many ways. I encourage you to take time to recall His goodness and thank Him like David did in Psalm 103:

> Bless the LORD, O my soul; and all that is within me, bless His holy name. Bless the LORD, O my soul, and forget none of His benefits (vv. 1–2).

The Lord expects us not only to enjoy His blessings, but also to express our gratitude to Him and openly give glory to God.

What about the hard times? Perhaps during this bygone year you can recall more trials, disappointments, sickness, loss and tears than blessings, and you have a hard time finding anything for which you could thank God. Yet as believers we are instructed to

> Rejoice always; pray without ceasing; in everything give thanks; for this is God's will for you in Christ Jesus (1 Thessalonians 5:16–18).

Does this Scripture mean that a mother is supposed to rejoice and thank God for losing her child to a terrible disease? Should a wife rejoice that her marriage is falling apart because her husband is an alcoholic?

No, that is *not at all* what this Scripture says! God Himself is deeply grieved by all the tragedy, sickness, pain and destruction His creation suffers because of the fall of man.

Rejoice always. When we take a closer look at this Bible passage, we discover that it only tells us that we are to *rejoice always.* It doesn't say at all that we should be shouting for joy over the bad things that befall us in this sinful and corrupt world. The apostle Paul clearly names the subject for our rejoicing:

> Rejoice **in the Lord** always; again I will say, rejoice! (Philippians 4:4).

Jesus is our reason for being able to rejoice, even when we shed tears in the midst of struggles and grief. It's a paradox the world will not understand. Our ability to experience joy *in* our trials comes from focusing our hearts on Jesus and what He has done for us.

Something wonderful happens when we begin to reflect on how Jesus laid down His life for our salvation, how He forgave our sin and wrote our names in the Book of Life, how He filled us with His Spirit and promised to come back to take us where He is.

Suddenly our hearts are comforted and lifted up in faith. We begin to recognize that our trials and pain are temporary, but our future is glorious and eternal. That's when we can rejoice in the Lord in truth.

In everything give thanks. This Scripture would indeed be nearly impossible for us to obey if it would require from us to thank God for the tragedy that our child is blind or that we are unable to feed our families. However, if we read it carefully it only instructs us to give thanks *in* everything. That means we should thank God *in the midst* of our difficult circumstances.

But what could we possibly thank God for if we are hurting and don't understand why all these disappointments and trials are happening to us?

The Bible gives us detailed instructions about the things for which we should thank God:

> *Give thanks to the LORD, for He is good; for His loving-kindness is everlasting* (Psalm 136:1).

Our knowledge and confession that God is eternally good, loving and kind—this is the rock we can stand on when nothing else makes sense. This truth tells us that we can trust our heavenly Father even in the most difficult times of our lives and that His thoughts are all good toward us. He alone knows the end from the beginning; one day we will recognize that He didn't make a single mistake when He said "no" to something or permitted us to go through a difficult trial.

It's Christmas. When God sent His Son to this world, He took all our fears away regarding His love for us. Let us love Him back by rejoicing in His gift and thanking Him for His loving-kindness.

May the Lord bless you and help you trust Him fully.

In Jesus,

Gisela

31 Redeeming Your Time

FEBRUARY 2004

Dear Sister,

Our family was able to spend Christmas and New Year's together at home, for which I am very grateful. Daniel and Sarah returned to India at the beginning of January, and my husband is right now traveling to various mission fields. I am working on my writing projects for the ministry, with the goal to finish some of them soon so I can travel as well.

God has graciously given all of us a new year to serve Him. In the light of our calling to win the lost world to the Lord Jesus Christ, I would like to share a few thoughts with you about the importance of using our time wisely.

God has given each of us a specific life span here on earth. As the Creator and author of life, only He knows how long it will be. Whether we live to be 20 years or 85, He is the One who made the decision on the number of our days.

*And in Thy book they were all written, the days that were
ordained for me, when as yet there was not one of them*
(Psalm 139:16).

The time God has given us is an incredible gift. Each day is
like a blank piece of paper, and God allows us to write on it whatever we wish. That means we are given the awesome opportunity
to turn our 24 hours into something that honors God and lasts for
eternity—or we can live for ourselves, the world and the devil.

The saddest thing is that most people, including Christians,
don't recognize the preciousness of time. They simply waste much
of it on meaningless things such as sitting around doing nothing,
idle talk and selfish living.

Time is the one thing in our lives we cannot replace. Once
an hour, day or year is past, we cannot go back and relive it. Our
life span is like a burning candle. It can only give off light until the
flame has consumed the wax.

The Bible clearly tells us that we have only *one* chance on this
earth to live for God and use the time and opportunities He has
entrusted to us. After our lives are over, He will require an account
of what we did with them:

*It is appointed for men to die once, and after this comes
judgment* (Hebrews 9:27).

Jesus lived an extremely time-conscious life in a society and
among people accustomed to the slow rural village style of living.
He made statements like these:

My hour has not yet come (John 2:4).

My time is at hand . . . (Matthew 26:18).

Where did His time-consciousness come from? It came from His understanding that God had a fixed timeline for this earth, for every human being and for His own life as Redeemer. Jesus knew He needed to exactly follow His Father's timetable in order to fulfill God's will and the prophecies regarding Himself.

It also filled His heart with an overwhelming urgency for the souls of men who were perishing and would be lost forever unless they could be reached with the Gospel in their lifetime. In the light of all this, Jesus could not afford to waste even an hour of His time or pursue His own interests.

Jesus wanted His disciples to be consumed with the same time-consciousness and urgency for the ripe harvest fields as He was. **This is what He said to them—and says to us today:**

> *We must work the works of Him who sent Me, as long as it is day; night is coming, when no man can work* (John 9:4).

> *Do you not say, "There are yet four months, and then comes the harvest"? Behold, I say to you, lift up your eyes, and look on the fields, that they are white for harvest* (John 4:35).

As followers and servants of Christ, let us examine our hearts to see whether we truly share His likeness in redeeming the precious time God gave to us on this earth.

Did you know that 30 minutes could make a huge difference for eternity? Every day 80,000 people of our generation die and face eternity, most of them never having heard the Gospel. Imagine what God could do to reach them if you and I would redeem just 30 minutes of our wasted time each day! In one week, each of us would gain 3 hours and 30 minutes to spend in intercession, witnessing and discipling others. In one month that would become 15 hours; and in one year, 182 hours and 30 minutes.

If all 7,500 sisters who receive my letter would do the same, God would have 1,368,750 extra hours of our time to invest in the salvation of the lost world. I have no doubt that multitudes would come to know Jesus as a result.

I want to challenge you at the beginning of this new year to take a good look at the way you spend your average day. Then make a decision before the Lord to daily redeem 30 minutes of your wasted or selfishly used time in building His kingdom.

The coming of Jesus is closer now than it ever has been. Let us use the time we have left in such a way that it will honor Him.

For the year 2004, let's pray and believe God together for:

• Continued freedom to share the Gospel.

• New open doors on every mission field.

• Protection for our church members, missionaries and Bible school students.

• Wisdom for our leaders.

• Faithfulness and humble hearts for everyone who is part of our GFA and Believers Church family.

With love and prayers,

Gisela

32 How Faithful Are You?

Dear Sister,

Yesterday while returning home from the grocery store, I was thinking about a Scripture in the New Testament. The master says to his slave, who had doubled the two talents he had received to work with, *"You were faithful with a few things; I will put you in charge of many things"* (Matthew 25:23).

Jesus told this story to illustrate how God decides which of His servants should receive greater responsibilities in His kingdom.

Many of us sincerely ask the Lord to use our lives in significant ways to bring glory to His name and build His work. Perhaps we pray that God will use us to win thousands of souls to Christ, see miracles happening through our ministry, bring our entire village to the Lord, lead a Gospel team, train others for ministry or become a Bible school teacher.

God may indeed be eager to answer all those prayers even far beyond what we asked for. Though His calling and gifts are purely given to us by His grace, when it comes to ministry and leading others, God looks for a specific Christlike character quality in our lives: faithfulness.

It would be irresponsible of God to blindly commit His work to us. That's why He told us through the apostle Paul: *". . . it is required of stewards that one be found trustworthy"* (1 Corinthians 4:2). Paul explains in the previous verse that we are servants of Christ and stewards of the mysteries of God.

This means God has entrusted the whole truth of the Gospel into our care and asked us to represent Him in this world. If we truly understand this responsibility, it should cause us to serve the Lord with fear and trembling. This is not because we are afraid of our heavenly Father, but because we know how easily our own hearts are willing to compromise the truth. Yet we are called to be ambassadors of Him whose very nature is faithfulness.

My dear Sister, before God can justify giving us the greater things we long for, we first *must* become trustworthy. Otherwise we surely will bring dishonor to the name of the Lord.

That's the reason He begins our ministry training by letting us practice faithfulness in the small things of daily life and our personal walk with Him. He watches and waits for our faithfulness to grow to a higher level before He adds more responsibilities to our service.

Jesus evaluates our trustworthiness by how faithful we are in the tiny things. When He told His disciples the story about the unrighteous steward, He concluded, *"He who is faithful in a* *very little thing is faithful also in much; and he who is unrighteous in a very little thing is unrighteous also in much"* (Luke 16:10).

Did you realize that Jesus didn't say, "He who is faithful in a *little* thing"? Instead, He said, ". . . in a *very little* thing"!

That means the Lord is evaluating our readiness for greater responsibility in His kingdom, not by considering our great ministry accomplishments and impressive Bible knowledge, but by examining our *very little* things.

He knows that most of our compromises in faithfulness are found in the very small things others can't see and that we consider insignificant. Yet to Him these tiny things are the *most accurate measurement* of where we truly are with our walk in truth and righteousness.

We must give importance to these very small things. Unless we deliberately deal with these areas of our lives, we ourselves hinder and delay God from using us in a more significant way. We must look carefully for the *very small* hidden things that until now we haven't taken seriously.

Yesterday, the Lord pointed one out in my life. My husband has several shirts that are more trouble to iron than the others he has. He likes some of his other shirts to be starched and pressed by the laundry service, but not these. Each time he puts them for washing, I hope he doesn't tell me to iron them myself. Until now, when he told me to iron them at home, I did it, but if he said nothing, I took them to the cleaners. Technically I didn't disobey him, but in my heart I knew he would have wanted me to do them at home. However, I had convinced myself that each time I was gaining two hours to work for the Lord.

In the light of these Scriptures about being faithful, I suddenly realized what I was doing, and I loudly said to myself, "God is testing my faithfulness with these shirts. How could I ever think that these two extra hours of ministry would amount to anything eternal?"

I am very sure this is not the only *very little thing* that needed correction in my life.

What about you, my dear Sister? Perhaps there is a tiny dishonesty in you when it comes to money, such as not giving back a few extra coins of change the lady at the marketplace gave you by mistake.

Maybe your *very little thing* is a touch of resentment or jealousy toward another sister.

Or it could be a very small disobedience to your husband or team leader, such as doing a task half a day later than you were supposed to.

It could be a slight exaggeration in your ministry report, a little pretense that makes others believe you are praying more than you actually do, a tiny deception by leaving out a few facts when you tell about an incident or a little bit of neglect in a responsibility committed to you.

Our motivation in dealing with our very little things must never be legalism or an attempt to become better than others. No, it must be our sincere desire to align our lives with the truth and become, through and through, trustworthy in the sight of God.

Let's pray for one another that each of us will surrender to the refining work the Holy Spirit wants to do in our lives in this area of faithfulness.

I love you in Jesus,

Gisela

33 What Is the Lord Teaching You?

June 2004

Dear Sister,

This letter comes to you from Germany. Three weeks ago, I had to leave in a hurry to come here because my mother was in the hospital and was not doing well. She is at her home now, but she can't do much and needs a lot of rest. My mother always liked to work in her house and garden, and apart from help with grocery shopping and harvesting fruit from her trees, she could do most things by herself. Last September she had an operation from which she recovered, but over the past few months she had problems again, and the doctors' prognosis is not good. However, many people are praying and believing with us for God to heal her.

These past few days I have been thinking about how God always uses the circumstances we are in to teach us something, and I was asking myself: What are the specific things God wants me to learn by coming here? I wrote down a few of them:

1. As my Lord, He has the right to change my timetable and my plans. Consequently, I ought to be totally at peace with His decision even if I don't know how long I need to stay here. My joy should be to please Him and not to feel sorry for myself over the things I don't get to do. That's the attitude Jesus had when He came to this earth.

These were the plans that changed for me:

- Two days before I had to leave, we celebrated the opening of our expanded GFA building in the USA, along with GFA's 25th anniversary.

- We had staff and leaders from different countries come for two weeks, and I was really looking forward to spending time with everybody, especially with the sisters from abroad.

- One of the leaders stayed in our home, and we planned for the others to visit us for fellowship and dinner. I wanted to cook and do some special things for our guests.

- Daniel and Sarah, our children, had also come home for a few weeks; and I hoped to take them shopping before they returned to India.

- On the 20th of May, my husband and I were going to celebrate our 30th wedding anniversary.

- Finally, I was going to do some more of my writing assignments and then travel with my husband to India for a few weeks.

I am glad to say that I am experiencing God's peace and am able to trust Him, even though much of my writing has been delayed.

2. The Lord wants me to realize that my mother is very important to Him. The things I do for her, such as cooking, cleaning and washing clothes, are opportunities to honor her and to serve Him. In fact, if I do these things *"as unto the Lord,"* then in His eyes they are ministry, just as much as the "real ministry" I am involved in with GFA.

3. Jesus wants me to encourage my mother to trust Him daily and to set her focus on eternal things, rather than on all the work she wants to do. My mother is nearly 90 years old, and from the health problems she experienced recently, she is afraid of what may happen to her in the days to come. I tell her that God never makes a mistake, His thoughts are all good toward her and she needs to trust Him one day at a time. I have asked her almost every day to read Psalm 139 and meditate on what it means in her situation.

I know that getting old and losing strength is not easy for anyone. However, I do remember the final years of my mother's older brother, who had become a believer. Several years before he died, he couldn't work on his farm any longer and had to spend much of his time in bed. Whenever we visited him, he was full of expectation and consumed with longing to see Jesus. All he wanted to talk about was Jesus and the glory of heaven that was soon awaiting him. His heart was in heaven long before he ever got there. It was beautiful to witness a child of God who was no longer clinging to this present world but whose whole affection was set on things above.

Experiencing now how difficult it is for my mother to let go of much of the work that had been so important to her all her life, I am learning that I must watch out that my own focus is, and remains, on eternal things (Colossians 3:1–2). Only then will I long to see Jesus face-to-face and look forward to heaven as my uncle did.

If our hearts can look beyond this present world, then when our earthly bodies grow older and weaker, we will not despair. Instead, we will regard the decrease of our strength as a signal that soon we will be clothed with our dwelling from heaven (2 Corinthians 5:2).

These are some of the things I talk about with my mother; and I read Scriptures to her to support my words.

My dear Sister, what is the Lord teaching you these days? Please take a good look at your wonderful or difficult circumstances and determine what you are learning. It's important to your spiritual development—and for your ministry—that you recognize clearly what God is teaching you. Perhaps you should write these things in a notebook so you won't forget.

The book of Psalms is such a notebook in which David, Asaph, the sons of Korah and many others expressed in poetic form what they were learning during the best, as well as the most trying, times of their lives. You will benefit greatly if you read through a few psalms today with the purpose of finding out what specific lessons God was teaching the writers. You will read amazing statements like these:

> *In Thy presence is fullness of joy* (Psalm 16:11).

> *For by Thee I can run upon a troop; and by my God I can leap over a wall* (Psalm 18:29).

> *For a day in Thy courts is better than a thousand outside* (Psalm 84:10).

> *It is good for me that I was afflicted, that I may learn Thy statutes* (Psalm 119:71).

God teaches all of us His eternal truth on a personal level. Let us be thankful to Him, even if the circumstances of our "classroom" are not what we would choose for ourselves.

May the love and grace of God be real to you today and always.

Your sister in Christ,

Gisela

34 Taking Your Place in God's Plan

AUGUST 2004

Dear Sister,

I am grateful that I can write this letter to you from home. A week after I returned from taking care of my mother in Germany, my husband had to leave for India. At present I don't know how soon I will need to return to be with my mother. For now, I am working on my GFA writing projects that are due within the next two months.

When I think about you and all the other sisters in our ministry, I praise God for the grace and calling He has given you to help win the unreached multitudes of Asia to the Lord Jesus Christ.

In this letter, I wish to help you see the task God gave you to do from His perspective.

Learn to see your ministry in the context of God's overall plan. Whether God asked you to encourage and help your husband, spend time in intercession for the mission fields or serve with a Gospel team, local church, GFA office or Bible college, you must learn to see your calling in the context of God's overall plan.

It would be a grave mistake to determine the level of your commitment to the task by how significant it looks to you or whether or not it is on your ministry "wish list." We are often so shortsighted and self-absorbed that we think no further than our own little world. Consequently, we act as if our ministry only affects ourselves and a few people around us. The truth is, we are part of an enormous plan God has for our own nations and the entire world. If we open our eyes, we will see that our little assignment is actually a piece of His overall strategy. Just read Matthew 28:18–20 and Acts 1:8.

God deals with us on two different levels. Very often our carelessness or resistance toward a ministry assignment comes from our lack of understanding of how God works. He relates and deals with us on two entirely different levels:

First, as individuals: *"You have received a spirit of adoption as sons by which we cry out, 'Abba! Father!'"* (Romans 8:15).

God is our heavenly Father, and we are His beloved children. As such, He treats us as individuals and has a personal relationship with each one. Our uniqueness is precious to Him, because He designed it. He knows and understands us like no one else; He loves, cares and works with each one of us on a very personal level. We enjoy the individual attention we get from Him, and we wish He would always deal with us in this manner.

Second, as part of the Body of Christ: *"For even as the body is one and yet has many members, and all the members of the body,* *though they are many, are one body, so also is Christ. For by one Spirit we were all baptized into one body . . ."* (1 Corinthians 12:12–13).

When it comes to church life and the ministry that flows out of it, God considers and treats us as an integrated part of a living organism: the Body of Christ. For this oneness with the whole body to become a working reality, it is necessary that we humble ourselves and allow God to melt down our independent self-life. Only when that happens are we able to see how interrelated and interdependently we should be functioning. That also puts our "insignificant"-looking ministry assignment in the right perspective. We suddenly realize how crucial our tiny contribution is to the effective fulfillment of God's overall plan for the Church and the lost world.

Often we resist this melting-down process and fight to keep our individuality intact. Consequently our ministry contribution is not freely available to the Body of Christ to accomplish God's purpose.

Your ministry is vital to the execution of God's plan and the growth of the Church.

> *From whom [Christ] the whole body, being fitted and held together by that which every joint supplies, according to the proper working of each individual part, causes the growth of the body for the building up of itself in love* (Ephesians 4:16).

To illustrate this Scripture, picture yourself, along with the task God entrusted to you, as if you were a tiny tooth on a little wheel in your watch. If you break off that tiny tooth, the little wheel can no longer accurately turn the bigger wheel next to it. That bigger wheel is designed to turn another and so on. The end result will be that the entire movement of your watch is affected, and it is unable to work precisely as it was designed to be.

In light of this, think about the implications your lack of dedication to your God-given assignment could directly have on your husband, team members, local church, GFA office, Bible college—and ultimately on the entire Believers Church movement and the lost world.

Dear Sister, please take seriously whatever God gave you to do and fulfill it with great faithfulness. When you get to heaven and see how important your contribution was in building His kingdom, you will be glad you did.

Let us unite our hearts in prayer for Brother Manja and his family in Nepal. On July 1, the Nepali Supreme Court upheld a guilty verdict in Pastor Manja's case. Our brother has already spent four years in prison for a crime he didn't commit.

- Pray and believe God for a miracle. He is well able to do so.

- Pray that the Lord will sustain Brother Manja, his wife and their two children by His grace.

- Pray that through their testimony and steadfastness, the Church in Nepal will grow.

May God's grace be with you.

I love you in Jesus,

Gisela

35

Trusting in God's Sovereignty

OCTOBER 2004

Dear Sister,

Just a few days after I wrote my last letter to you, I had to return to Germany in a hurry because my mother's health was rapidly declining. Four weeks later, she went to be with the Lord. It was very sad for all of us to see Mom's strength and ability to care for herself fading away. Even though she was very weak, she still was able to get up with our help until two days before she died.

During her final week on earth, she slept most of the day. When she woke up, she often felt disoriented. Both were the result of toxins accumulating in her body due to her illness. However, in between she had some good hours where she could drink her afternoon tea with my sister and me and enjoy looking at her garden with all the beautiful trees, flowers and birds. These are now precious memories I will always treasure.

Every day I took time to pray with my mother and read the Bible to her. One day when she expressed that she felt that she might have to die soon, I sat down at her bedside and asked her plainly: "Mom, if the Lord wants to call you home soon, would you be ready? Do you know that your sins are forgiven and that you will go to heaven?" She answered that she was sure of her salvation. I then asked her if she needed to forgive anyone or if there was anything she still needed to make right. She said that there was nothing she had to bring in order.

Mom had some questions about dying. So I read and explained the Scriptures to her that dealt with being absent from the body and present with the Lord, that talk about the new body God will clothe us with and that say He will wipe away all our tears. I also told her that for a believer, death is just like walking through a door into the presence of God, and when the Lord called her home, Jesus would walk with her through this door and hold her hand. One afternoon when she felt especially good, we listened together to a teaching tape about heaven, which gave her much peace.

During those last few days when Mom was so deeply asleep, I would play hymns for her on the piano or sit at her bedside, hold her hand and just read Scripture to her and pray. Though she didn't react outwardly, I was certain that the Word of God would strengthen her spirit. The morning Mom went to be with the Lord, my sister and her family and I were with her. We held her, prayed with her and told her we loved her. Just before Jesus took her home, she looked at each one of us and smiled.

The funeral and all the arrangements were emotionally draining. Perhaps the most painful moment was when Mom's body was taken from her home and we knew she would never come back. I was glad Daniel and Sarah came from India to be with me at the funeral. It encouraged me a lot.

Death is indeed a cruel enemy. But praise God for the victory over death that is ours in Jesus. There are two things I would like to share with you from this trying time:

1. God's sovereignty is always for good and never for evil. I kept this statement on a piece of paper in my Bible. I often read and thought about it as I watched my mother's health deteriorate. This declaration is based on Scriptures such as Jeremiah 29:11, Psalm 136:1, Psalm 139:17 and 1 John 4:8.

There are things I don't understand about my mother's life. Why did she have to deal with this sickness at age 89—robbed of her strength, hospitalized four times and twice operated on? Why was she not allowed to live her final year in peace, enjoying her family and her garden? And why did God choose not to heal her miraculously as He is well able to do and for which we also prayed and believed?

The answers to these questions are only found in the infinite wisdom of God's heart and in His everlasting love, neither of which I can even remotely comprehend here on earth. But I experienced how peace filled my heart as I trusted in God's sovereignty, knowing that it is always for good and never for evil. This has enabled me to put my questions on hold until eternity. Perhaps this is something you can use someday when you too have unanswered questions.

2. There are so many things I can thank and honor God for, even in the midst of grief, if I open my eyes to the grace and goodness of God that surrounded my mother's homegoing:

- I know that my mother went to be with Jesus and that I will see her again.

- Though she was very sick, she had no pain.

- We had her with us until she was nearly 90.

- She was able to stay and die in her own home as she had always wished.

- We were with her when she passed away.

- The Lord sent me back to Germany at the right time.

- He gave me enough physical strength to take care of Mom even though I slept very little.

- My heart was at peace even in the most difficult hours.

- The Lord kept me awake during the early morning hours of Mom's final day and helped me notice the change in her condition. Thus I could call my sister and her family to come in time.

- Thousands of people prayed for Mom and our family. I certainly felt their prayers.

- Daniel and Sarah visited their grandma a month earlier, on their way to India.

- My husband was able to see Mom one week before she died while stopping on his journey home.

- I had the opportunity to share the Gospel very clearly with some unsaved relatives and friends.

I have found that it really helps to make a list of the loving care and kind acts of God when I face sadness or trials. Try it for yourself. You will come away with a new perspective and a grateful heart.

I want to thank you for praying for my mother's health this past year. God answered and took her home. Now she is completely well and rejoicing in His presence. Today (September 11) would have been her 90th birthday.

When I told her a few months ago that thousands of missionary sisters in Asia and other places were praying for her, she was deeply touched and wanted me to thank you on her behalf. Dear Sister, you are a blessing!

I love you in Jesus,

Gisela

36 Living in the Light of God's Faithfulness

DECEMBER 2004

Dear Sister,

By the time you receive this letter, I will have traveled to India for most of December and part of January. I will enjoy the students' Christmas program at the ABS, meet our leaders during their mid-December meeting and spend Christmas and New Year's together with my family.

When I think about the birth of our Savior, I believe we Christians celebrate the greatest and most joyous holiday in the entire world. God's incredible love gave us His only Son as a gift so He could die for our sin and we could live forever.

God's amazing grace and His faithfulness to His Word were never more visible than when Jesus was born in Bethlehem 2,000 years ago.

This Christmas season, I would like you to join me in reflecting on God's faithfulness as it relates to the Christmas story. I believe it will cause your faith to grow as a result.

God never made a promise He didn't intend to keep. Right after Adam and Eve sinned, God gave them the first promise about a coming Savior. If God had no intentions to send Jesus, He simply could have let the knowledge about His promise die out with Adam or Noah. Instead, He took it upon Himself to keep this promise alive by repeating it to Abraham and to the many generations after him.

When God made His promise, He also had a plan. God knew all along that Adam and Eve would sin and mankind would need a Redeemer. Therefore, He had His plan of salvation in place before He ever created men:

> *You were not redeemed with perishable things . . . but with precious blood, as of a lamb . . . the blood of Christ. For He [Jesus] was foreknown before the foundation of the world* (1 Peter 1:18–20).

> *. . . the Lamb slain from the foundation of the world* (Revelation 13:8, NKJV).

God was well able to preserve His promise during the darkest hours of human history. Mankind came close to extinction in Noah's flood because of their violence and corruption. Only Noah and his family were brought safely through. God preserved the promise of a Savior through this one family that believed in Him.

It didn't take long for the generations that followed to forget the living God and worship idols. God had to start all over to reveal Himself to Abraham and give him the promise He had previously made to Adam and Eve regarding the Savior, who was going to be one of Abraham's descendants.

God preserved the human family line through which Jesus would be born through 400 years of slavery in Egypt, 40 years of wilderness travel, countless wars and 70 years of exile in Babylon.

He did not go back on His Word or alter His promise as time went by. To do so would have been totally inconsistent with His righteous nature. To help Abraham and us be steadfast in our faith, He reinforced His promise with an oath:

> *In the same way God, desiring even more to show to the heirs of the promise the unchangeableness of His purpose, interposed with an oath, so that by two unchangeable things in which it is impossible for God to lie, we who have taken refuge would have strong encouragement to take hold of the hope set before us* (Hebrews 6:17–18, NKJV).

Even when His people were unfaithful, God remained faithful to His Word. How many times did the people of Israel turn their backs on God and break their covenant with Him! Yet God remained faithful and kept His part of the covenant (see Psalm 89:30–34). He forgave them a thousand times and brought them back to Himself. Most of all, He never withdrew His promise to send them the Savior.

He orchestrated people and circumstances in such a way that every detail of His promise was fulfilled. Just for Jesus to be born in the city of David as God foretold, He set the whole Roman Empire in motion by inspiring Caesar Augustus to take a census. This required everyone to travel to their ancestral home, including Mary and Joseph.

What does all this mean to us?

It means that the faithfulness of God to His Word is still the same, because God does not change.

It means He has a plan for each of us.

And it means He is committed and able to fulfill every promise He spoke in the Scripture regarding our lives, our children, our ministry and our future. Even our failures and difficult circumstances are no hindrance for Him to accomplish what He said He would do.

All God needs from us is for us to trust Him, just as Noah, Abraham, and Mary and Joseph did. He will work out the rest and securely bring it to pass. And this will calm our hearts and give us peace in the midst of a flood and a world of uncertainties.

My dear Sister, my prayer and Christmas wish for you is that you live your life more and more in the light of God's faithfulness.

Please pray with us for our 370 Bridge of Hope primary schools:

- For God's grace to educate and care for the 19,200 children enrolled in our schools.

- For each child, and his or her family, to come to know Jesus personally.

- For our teachers to be filled with the love of Christ.

- For God to enable us to open many more schools by next June.

May the knowledge of God's faithfulness fill your heart with joy this Christmas and every day of the new year.

Your sister in Christ,

Gisela

37 Are You Moved with Compassion?

FEBRUARY 2005

Dear Sister,

When my letter arrives at your home, it will be nearly two months since the tsunami devastated so many coastal areas in Southeast Asia and even Africa.

Through the videos, pictures and reports of the news media, the whole world witnessed a catastrophe unparalleled in our lifetime. More than 160,000 people lost their lives, and the horrendous devastation of the tsunami also wiped out the homes and livelihoods of millions of others.

The suffering and unbearable pain and agony of the survivors was brought near to us in their stories: Parents unable to hold on to their children when the waves came . . . family members seeing their loved ones swept away by the floodwaters ... people severely injured or buried alive under collapsed buildings ... children wandering about lost and crying for their parents who perished ... survivors searching among the dead bodies for their parents, spouses, brothers, sisters, sons and daughters ... mass graves and mourning without end.

Thank God for the many countries, organizations and individuals that have come together to help with emergency and relief operations. For the survivors, it will take years to rebuild their homes and communities. Even then, their lives will never be the same. Nothing can bring back the dear ones they lost in the flood.

I write this letter during the second week of January. A few days, ago my husband and other Believers Church leaders traveled to Sri Lanka and the coastal areas of India to visit the devastated areas and see the relief work Believers Church is doing in these places. In Sri Lanka we are temporarily sheltering 10,000 children in 10 camps and caring for other tsunami victims as well who lost everything. We are also distributing food, water, medicine and other emergency supplies in hard-hit communities. Plans are already under way to reconstruct homes and equip families with tools that will enable them to once again earn their livelihood.

Shortly after the tsunami hit, my husband sent a letter to all our churches to encourage the believers to contribute to the relief fund. I am so glad God is using Believers Church to practically help these desperate people and, at the same time, share His love and compassion with them.

Compassion is so central to the Gospel message and to the heart of God that we as believers will not be able to represent Christ without it.

Even the very name of God reveals that compassion is part of His nature:

Then the LORD passed by in front of him [Moses] and proclaimed, "The LORD, the LORD God, compassionate and gracious, slow to anger, and abounding in lovingkindness and truth" (Exodus 34:6).

The Lord Jesus is *"the exact representation of His [God the Father's] nature"* (Hebrews 1:3). While He was on earth, Jesus' ministry was marked by deep compassion for the people He encountered. The concern He showed for the lost and suffering—the tears He wept for them, the kindness He showed them and the tenderness with which He treated them—all came genuinely from His heart:

And seeing the multitudes, He felt compassion for them, because they were distressed and downcast like sheep without a shepherd (Matthew 9:36).

And when He came out, He saw a great multitude, and felt compassion for them, and healed their sick (Matthew 14:14).

And behold, two blind men ... cried out, saying, "Lord, have mercy on us, Son of David!" ... And moved with compassion, Jesus touched their eyes; and immediately they received their sight (Matthew 20:30–34).

And a leper came to Him. ... And moved with compassion, He stretched out His hand and touched him, and said to him, "I am willing; be cleansed" (Mark 1:40–41).

... a dead man was being carried out, the only son of his mother, and she was a widow; ... And when the Lord saw her, He felt compassion for her, and said to her, "Do not weep." ... And He said, "Young man, I say to you, arise!" ... And Jesus gave him back to his mother (Luke 7:12–15).

When Jesus therefore saw her weeping, and the Jews who came with her, also weeping, He was deeply moved in spirit, and was troubled. . . . Jesus wept. . . . Jesus therefore again being deeply moved within, came to the tomb. . . . He cried out with a loud voice, "Lazarus, come forth." He who had died came forth (John 11:33–44).

Our calling is to live in this world as Jesus lived:

. . . walk in the same manner as He walked (1 John 2:6).

. . . because as He is, so also are we in this world (1 John 4:17).

That means we must *"put on a heart of compassion"* (Colossians 3:12) just like Jesus had toward others. It is possible for us to do so, because we share His nature through our new birth. Then we will weep His tears for the tsunami victims, touch them with His hands, comfort them with His tenderness, and help them with His generosity and love. And then the world will see Jesus lifted up.

Let us pray together for the tsunami victims as if they were our own family members, and let us also remember the other needs related to this tragedy:

- For the survivors—for God's comfort in their pain, for His provision for their needs and for their salvation.

- For all the countries and organizations involved in relief and reconstruction operations.

- For the relief work and ministry among the survivors done by Believers Church.

- That our churches and believers will participate with generosity and eagerness in helping the survivors.

May the Lord Jesus bless you and keep you close to Himself.

Your sister in Christ,

Gisela

38 Your Influence as a Woman

APRIL 2005

Dear Sister,

In February our Believers Church leadership called 25 sisters from several countries for the first Believers Church Synod Consultation on Women's Ministry.

We met at the Gospel for Asia Biblical Seminary campus in Kerala, India, and for five days we prayed for and discussed the future of our Believers Church women's ministry. We worked on an overall strategy that would unify and strengthen the women's fellowships in all our churches and give them common goals and clear direction for their meetings and ministry.

In the end, we compiled all our ideas and recommendations and submitted them to the Believers Church Executive Council for their consideration and decision.

Though we were very busy, we had a wonderful time of fellowship, and everyone participated and contributed.

Sister Sarah (my daughter) and Sister Athonuo, who are in charge of the girls' hostel and who also took part in the consultation, hosted the meeting in the girls' chapel. They also made the arrangements for our stay and supplied us with tea, coffee, snacks and everything else we needed. Their hospitality was a real blessing to everyone.

The closing session ended with my husband speaking to the campus community and the delegates about the importance of women's role in the local church and in missions. I hope his message will come out in a booklet. It would greatly motivate our pastors and churches to encourage the sisters in their devotion and service to the Lord.

I would like to share with you a few thoughts on the influence we have as sisters.

Our influence as women is much greater than we think. Even if we never do or say anything publicly, we still have enormous power to influence those around us for good or bad with our behavior, values, attitude and words. This is especially true in regard to our families.

1. Our influence as wives:

Consider the influence Queen Jezebel had on her husband, King Ahab. Even prior to his marriage, Ahab's testimony before God was bad: *"Ahab the son of Omri did evil in the sight of the LORD more than all who were before him"* (1 Kings 16:30).

However, Ahab's bent toward evil turned into a landslide of corruption and idolatry after he got married, and the Bible gives us the reason why: *"Surely there was no one like Ahab who sold himself to do evil in the sight of the LORD, because Jezebel his wife incited him"* (1 Kings 21:25).

Consider the influence Queen Esther had on her husband, King Ahasuerus. Ahasuerus was a pagan king who knew little or nothing about the true and living God. His right-hand man Haman had tricked him into signing a decree that would destroy the Jews throughout his kingdom.

Queen Esther, who never had a choice regarding her marriage to the king, was a godly young Jewish woman. She trusted in the Lord, prayed, fasted and put her life on the line to save her people. She approached her husband with respect, humility and wisdom. And through Esther's positive influence on her husband, the Jews were saved and wicked Haman was killed, along with many other enemies of the Jews. Mordecai, Esther's cousin who was a righteous man and loyal to the king, became his second in command. Ahasuerus finally had a man he could trust and who was guided by the wisdom of God.

What is your influence on your husband? So many times in the ministry, leaders, missionaries and pastors end up making compromises in following and serving the Lord because they were influenced by their wives' self-centered attitudes. On the other hand, a godly woman's attitude and words can encourage and strengthen her husband's walk with God in such a positive way that his service for the Lord is greatly blessed and multiplies.

2. Our influence as mothers:

The following proverb expresses accurately a mother's powerful influence in the lives of her children: *"The hand that rocks the cradle rules the world."*

Mothers mold their children more than anyone else, because during the formative years they are almost constantly together. To a great extent, mothers determine the future of the next generation by what they transfer to their children from their own lives.

Consider Jezebel's influence on the next two generations. Athaliah, Ahab and Jezebel's daughter, got married to King Jehoram of Judah. She turned out just like her mother, influencing her husband toward evil. Consequently God said about Jehoram: *"He walked in the way of the kings of Israel, just as the house of Ahab did (for Ahab's daughter was his wife), and he did evil in the sight of the LORD"* (2 Chronicles 21:6).

Then Ahaziah, Jehoram and Athaliah's son (and Jezebel's grandson), became king, and the Bible records: *"He also walked in the ways of the house of Ahab, for his mother was his counselor to do wickedly. And he did evil in the sight of the LORD like the house of Ahab, for they were his counselors after the death of his father, to his destruction"* (2 Chronicles 22:3–4).

Consider Lois's influence on the next two generations. Lois was a woman of sincere faith, who passed on the same quality of faith to her daughter Eunice who passed it on to her son Timothy. The apostle Paul wrote about them in his letter to Timothy: *"For I am mindful of the sincere faith within you, which first dwelt in your grandmother Lois, and your mother Eunice, and I am sure that it is in you as well"* (2 Timothy 1:5).

Timothy became the apostle Paul's true son in the faith, his most trusted and faithful co-worker and the one whom he left in charge of his life's work before he was martyred.

What is your influence on your children? Whether we are aware of it or not, as mothers we influence our children's future and spiritual life the most by what we are ourselves. The atmosphere we create in our homes and even our silent attitudes will shape their lives. Therefore let us be careful and diligent to walk according to the Word of God.

Let us pray together for our leader Brother Thomas, his wife, Kimchong, and their family. They recently lost their younger son due to a tragic motorcycle accident. Pray that the Lord will comfort them.

In Christ's love,

Gisela

39

You Were Bought with a Price

June 2005

Dear Sister,

Since I wrote to you last, some changes have happened in our family. Our son, Daniel, got married to Erika, a dear girl who has a heart for the Lord and for missions. The wedding was held in Kerala on our ABS campus, and my husband conducted the marriage ceremony. Most of our Believers Church leaders were there, and they all gathered around Daniel and Erika and prayed for God's blessing on their marriage. Daniel and Erika are serving the Lord together in India.

Now I have the opportunity to learn how to be a mother-in-law. My desire is that God would help me be an encouragement to my daughter-in-law.

Sarah, our daughter, came home for a few weeks during the ABS summer break. We had such a wonderful time together. She was sewing for both of us, planting flowers and trees in our garden and preparing herself for the new school year. Sarah will be teaching this year and also helping with the administration. These are new challenges for her, and she would surely appreciate your prayers. I miss her a lot since she returned to India, but I am thankful for all the nice memories of her visit.

Believers Church Women's Fellowship update. In April the Believers Church Executive Council reviewed and approved the proposal for the Believers Church Women's Fellowship program. The next step is to create a handbook for the Women's Fellowship and translate it into all the major languages. Right now this work is in progress.

Then all that remains is to set up the Women's Fellowship program in all the Believers Churches of every country where we work. This will be done by Believers Church women missionaries, students from our women's Bible schools and sisters' teams. Some of our Believers Church sisters and leaders' wives will coordinate the initial setup in each state and district.

To help with the necessary training, I will be traveling for at least two months in India and will also visit several of the neighboring countries.

My dear Sister, I count on you and all the other sisters who receive my letter to pray much for the ongoing preparations and for success in setting up the Women's Fellowship program.

There is no doubt in my mind that the Lord intends to make the Women's Fellowship a great blessing for Believers Church and for reaching the lost. I sincerely hope that you will want to be part of the Women's Fellowship in your own church.

How is your commitment to the Lordship of Christ? I want to conclude this letter with a little reality check you can do to help you find out how far you have come in making Jesus the Lord of your life.

The Bible tells us that we are not our own, but that Christ purchased us with His own blood and we have become God's own possession (1 Corinthians 6:19–20; 1 Peter 1:18–19; 1 Peter 2:9).

If these Scriptures are true of us, we will:

- Love what God loves and hate what He hates.

- Not question His Word.

- Be willing to lay down our own plans and wishes and submit to His.

- Have no resentment in our hearts when God sends us to a place we don't like to go.

- Be content with whatever He provides for us, whether little or much.

- Accept the lowest assignment with the same glad attitude as the highest.

- Do our best for Him with all our heart, all our soul and all our strength.

- Not ask for an easier or more comfortable life.

- Always seek to please Him instead of ourselves.

- Choose to serve others instead of ruling over them.

- Be satisfied with God's approval and not be affected by people's opinion of us.

- Walk in humility toward God and our brothers and sisters.

- Not seek—even secretly—for honor, position or recognition for our service.

- Be willing to suffer if it brings glory to Jesus and advances His kingdom.

- Never consider stopping our service to the Lord when other believers or leaders fail us.

- Find our fulfillment in obedience to His will instead of in the things we want to do.

- Place no restrictions on what God can do with our lives.

Please join us in prayer for:

- The development of the Believers Church Women's Fellowship program.

- The creation and translation of resources.

- The training of the sisters who will set up the program.

- The participation of the sisters in all our Believers Churches.

My dear Sister, may God's love and grace be with you as you live for Jesus and serve Him.

With love and prayers,

Gisela

40 What Causes God to Move?

AUGUST 2005

Dear Sister,

I am writing to you from Kolkata, India. Yesterday we finished our third Women's Fellowship training seminar. We still have four more to go to cover all the regions of India.

Sister Jeena is traveling with me. She is an ABS graduate and is working with her husband in the Indian state of Tripura. She is leading the discussion, planning and implementing sessions while I am teaching on the Women's Fellowship program. Because she speaks Hindi, she is able to interact with the sisters and make sure they understand the Women's Fellowship program.

We are very much encouraged by the enthusiasm and participation of the sisters from the different regions, and we are grateful for the support of our Believers Church leadership.

We have finalized the Women's Fellowship manual, and in a few days it will go for translation and printing. By the end of the rainy season, the sisters should have it in their hands and start setting up the Women's Fellowship program in the local churches.

During this trip, we are seeking to learn more about our sisters in the local churches: their education level, their social and economic situation and their involvement in the church and in missions.

So far we have learned that most of the sisters in our churches are very eager to live for the Lord and to serve Him. However, one of the greatest challenges our Women's Fellowship program will face is the illiteracy rate among the sisters in many parts of the country.

During these first three seminars, some of our major discussions centered on the question, "How can we implement the Women's Fellowship program in churches where very few sisters—and sometimes not even one—can read and write?"

It is clear to us that if we want our sisters to grow spiritually, we need to enable them to read and know the Word of God. That means we must create resources for our illiterate sisters and at the same time make it our priority to help them become literate. This will be a massive effort, especially because our churches are growing very fast. But I believe with all my heart that it can be done and must be done.

We have many ideas how the Women's Fellowship could accomplish this huge task, but so far our ideas are only on paper. They will need to come out of our notebooks and be translated into action. For that to happen, we need God to go before us and do no less of a miracle than when He parted the Red Sea.

I believe our heavenly Father is on our side with this vision, because He is much more concerned than any one of us that all His people know His Word so they can live by it.

What will motivate God to go before us and do miracles on our behalf? God will not be moved to action by the need and concern we feel for our sisters to become literate. He will not respond because we have plans and ideas or because we pray and shed tears, though all these things are important.

The Bible clearly teaches us that there is only one thing that pleases God and motivates Him to act on our behalf, and that is our faith:

> *And without faith it is impossible to please Him* (Hebrews 11:6).

> *But let him ask in faith without any doubting, for the one who doubts is like the surf of the sea driven and tossed by the wind. For let not that man expect that he will receive anything from the Lord* (James 1:6–7).

Jesus said to His disciples,

> *If you have faith as a mustard seed, you shall say to this mountain, "Move from here to there," and it shall move; and nothing shall be impossible to you* (Matthew 17:20).

He also said to Martha the sister of Lazarus, who had been dead for four days:

> *Did I not say to you, if you believe, you will see the glory of God?* (John 11:40).

Let us decide together to look not at the hugeness of the task, but rather at our God, with whom all things are possible.

Our Women's Fellowship program is just getting started with the initial training of the Women's Fellowship teams in our local churches. There is much to be done to develop the program, and we need God's guidance for each step. Please pray especially for God's wisdom in the area of literacy training. The task before us is huge, but I am excited and confident that we will succeed, because we trust in the living God whose love and power have no limits.

As for me, I have decided to read Hebrews 11 often in order to help my faith grow for our Women's Fellowship.

Besides honoring the Lord with our faith, let us also be available to Him with our time, gifts and training to serve our sisters through the Women's Fellowship program.

May the Lord encourage you today with His love and grace.

Your sister in Christ,

Gisela

41 All Things Contribute to God's Purpose for You

OCTOBER 2005

Dear Sister,

It is a privilege to write to you! This time my letter comes to you from home.

During July and August, Sister Jeena and I completed eight Believers Church Women's Fellowship training seminars in different parts of India. By the time you get this letter, we will be on our way to some of the neighboring countries for the same purpose. We certainly would appreciate your prayers.

As I write to you every other month, I often wonder how you are doing in your team or family life, your ministry and your personal walk with the Lord.

Perhaps over the past few months all your expectations were fulfilled, all your prayers were answered and now you are greatly encouraged in following the Lord. Or perhaps things didn't go so well, and much of what you had hoped and believed for has turned out different than you imagined. Maybe you have encountered so many difficulties and trials that you are asking yourself whether God's plan and purpose for your life will ever be fulfilled.

The apostle Paul wrote the answer to this question in his letter to the Roman Christians.

We are called according to God's purpose: *"And we know that God causes all things to work together for good to those who love God, to those who are called according to His purpose"* (Romans 8:28).

This Scripture tells us that if we are born again, we are automatically called according to God's purpose. That means He has something specific in mind that He wants to accomplish in each of us.

What is God's purpose for our lives? As believers, our goals are so many. We wish to be used of God, do something significant for His kingdom, have spiritual gifts, experience God's blessing and receive answers to our prayers. All these are wonderful goals—and biblical ones.

However, there is one thing God desires for His children more than anything else. It is His number-one purpose for our lives, and He decreed it before we were ever created: *"For whom He foreknew, He also predestined to become conformed to the image of His Son . . ."* (Romans 8:29).

This means that we are supposed to become everything Jesus is. His character, love, holiness, obedience, submission, servant attitude and heart for the lost are to be in us.

We are on our way. The word "become" in Romans 8:29 indicates that we are not yet there, but we are on our way. Every day, Christ's image is to increase and become more visible in our lives until the Lord Jesus is clearly seen in all we are and all we do. This will bring the greatest honor to our heavenly Father, much more than any accomplishment we could achieve in our life and ministry.

God causes all things to contribute to His purpose for us. *"And we know that God causes all things to work together for good to those who love God, to those who are called according to His purpose"* (Romans 8:28).

God turns *all* things in our lives—the good, the bad, Satan's attacks and even our failures—into opportunities for us to grow spiritually, to learn important lessons, to know Him better and to cling to Him in faith. The result will be that each time, we become a little more conformed into the image of Christ.

The life of Joseph in the Old Testament is a perfect example of how God causes even the worst things over which we have no control to become stepping-stones toward His purpose. Joseph faced the ordeals of being thrown in a well, being sold by his brothers and spending the best years of his life as a slave and prisoner; but it did not make him bitter, hopeless or cause him to give up on God's purpose for him.

On the contrary, he became strong in faith, learned valuable lessons and skills for his future, honored God in every situation and was convinced that nothing and no one could hinder God's plan for his life. That's why he could forgive his brothers and declare:

> And as for you, you meant evil against me, but God meant it for good (Genesis 50:20).

If we truly believe that God causes all things to work together for good in our lives, we will have peace in the midst of our storms. We will be able to see, by faith, God's purpose accomplished in our lives—no matter how many adversities we encounter on our journey. Most of all, we will allow God to use each trial to conform us closer to the image of His Son.

Let us pray together for the 20 *Athmik Yathra* radio rallies being held during December and January:

- The preparations.

- Attendance and safety.

- Thousands to receive Jesus.

- Follow-up and church planting.

My dear Sister, may the Lord encourage you today with His presence and love.

In Jesus,

Gisela

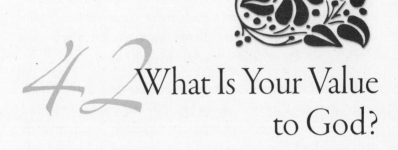

42 What Is Your Value to God?

DECEMBER 2005

Dear Sister,

It is Christmas, and I wish you God's blessing and peace. May the Lord touch your heart afresh with His love, which you have received in the gift of His Son Jesus.

This Christmas, take time to think about what it cost God the Father to send His only Son to this earth for our redemption. How His heart must have hurt to let Jesus go to live and suffer in a world—and among people—ravaged by sin and death and, in the end, to see Him go to the cross and die for our sin.

God could have easily intervened and spared Him from suffering such a cruel death, but because of His great love for us, He didn't. Do you realize how important and precious you are to Him?

What is our real value? Even as Christians, we often feel so insignificant and of little value to God, the church, our family and the world. But nothing could be further from the truth of God's Word!

When we read the Christmas story, we discover that our value is not at all determined by what the devil whispers into our ears, what other people say about us, our accomplishments or what we think about ourselves. God Himself declared our real value to the whole universe when He gave His only begotten Son to be born as a baby and by the price Jesus paid for us at the cross.

We need to adopt God's value toward ourselves and others. If we do, it will deliver us from our low self-image and self-pity and from the lies of the devil that say we are worthless. It will empower us to walk as children of God and to freely accept and enjoy God's love toward us.

Adopting God's value toward us will also revolutionize how we treat others. We will no longer evaluate them by their social status but consider them precious and worthy of our love, time and care. Most of all, it will motivate us to win them for Jesus.

I pray that this Christmas, God's love and the understanding of your worth to Him will transform your heart and fill you with great joy.

Women's Fellowship update. During the month of October, Sister Jeena and I held two Women's Fellowship training seminars in Nepal and Bangladesh. We truly felt privileged to be with our sisters there and to encourage them in starting the Women's Fellowship program in the Believers Churches of their countries.

Also, I was so happy and blessed that my daughter, Sarah, was able to come with us to Nepal. Many times I miss her very much, and I am so grateful to the Lord that I could spend a week with her.

In August, I wrote to you about the need for the Women's Fellowship to start literacy programs for our illiterate sisters in Believers Churches. Sister Jeena and I were so excited to hear the first success story from a Believers Church Women's Fellowship in Delhi, India.

After our training seminar in August, Sister Mini, the wife of our regional overseer Brother Simon, went to visit the Women's Fellowship groups that started in September in our churches in Delhi. In one of the churches, she found that 6 out of 12 sisters were illiterate. She challenged and encouraged the ones who could read to take the responsibility of teaching the others.

They took her exhortation seriously, and one sister began to meet with the illiterate women every day after work. She taught them and helped them practice the alphabets and read verses from the Bible. But her job didn't allow her to continue, so another sister, Mira, took over the teaching.

You know what happened? Within one month, all six sisters were able to read the Bible. They read slowly at first but improved with each day.

We met with Sister Mira, along with her pastor and his wife. She told us that most of the sisters she is teaching work as servants and are poor.

One of the former illiterate sisters was the pastor's wife. She had brought her Bible, and she read a passage to show us how she could read now. We were impressed with how well she read after only three months. I thought Sister Mira must be a college graduate or a teacher to be so successful in helping these sisters become literate. How surprised I was when I learned that she only had a fourth-grade education and was working as a servant in a home. On her own she had worked to improve some of the skills she had learned at school.

This dear sister allowed the Lord to put a burden and a vision in her heart for the illiterate sisters in her church. How I praise God for His grace that enabled her to succeed.

I believe God wants to challenge and encourage us with this story. If He can use a sister with a fourth-grade education, then He surely can use the many high school and college graduates and the professional women in our Believers Churches to help our illiterate sisters learn to read. What God is looking for are ladies with a willing heart who truly love their fellow sisters enough to invest their time to teach them literacy so that they, too, can read the Bible.

This Christmas, let us thank God for His great love and for all He has done:

- In our personal lives.

- In our families and churches.

- For the many prayers He has answered.

- For thousands of new believers in our churches.

- For His grace and promise to complete the work He started in us.

My dear Sister, may God's presence be with you always.

I love you in Jesus,

Gisela

BOOKS BY
GISELA YOHANNAN

BROKEN FOR A PURPOSE

Drawing from her own walk with the Lord, Gisela Yohannan shares how to find strength in God's presence and overcome seasons of testing so that Christ's life flows through you.

CONSIDER YOUR CALL

It is God's desire that we understand the joy and seriousness of our call to serve Him. In this book, Gisela Yohannan encourages us to run the race in such a way that we may win the prize.

DEAR SISTER

You will find hope and encouragement in this compilation of letters written by Gisela Yohannan over a seven-year period. She writes of the Lord's faithfulness through the events in her life and ministry—and how you can experience the promise of a new beginning as you walk with Jesus.

Order online at *www.gfa.org*

 GOSPEL FOR ASIA

After 2,000 years of Christianity, how can it be that nearly 3 billion people are still unreached with the Gospel? How long must they wait?

This is why Gospel for Asia exists.

More than 25 years ago, God specifically called us to invest our lives to reach the most unreached of South Asia through training and sending out national missionaries.

Gospel for Asia (GFA) is a missions organization dedicated to reaching the most unreached in the 10/40 Window. Thousands of GFA-supported pastors and missionaries serve full-time to share the love of Christ in 10 Asian countries.

National missionaries are highly effective because they work in their own or a similar culture. They already know, or easily learn, the language, customs and culture of the people to whom they minister. They don't need visas, and they live economically at the same level as their neighbors. These advantages make them one of the fastest and most effective ways to get the Gospel to the millions who are still waiting to hear.

However, the young, economically weak Asian Church and her missionaries can't do it alone. The enormous task of reaching nearly 3 billion people takes the help of the whole Body of Christ worldwide.

That is why GFA offers those who cannot go themselves the opportunity to become senders and prayer partners of national missionaries—together fulfilling the Great Commission and sharing in the eternal harvest of souls.

To find out more information about Gospel for Asia or to receive a free copy of K.P. Yohannan's best-selling book *Revolution in World Missions,* visit our website at www.gfa.org or contact one of our offices near you.

AUSTRALIA P.O. Box 3587, Village Fair, Toowoomba QLD 4350
 Freephone: 1300 889 339   Email: infoaust@gfa.org

CANADA 245 King Street E, Stoney Creek, ON L8G 1L9
 Toll free: 1-888-WIN-ASIA   Email: infocanada@gfa.org

GERMANY Postfach 13 60, 79603 Rheinfelden (Baden)
 Phone: 07623 79 74 77   Email: infogermany@gfa.org

KOREA Seok-Am Blg 5th floor, 6-9 Tereran-ro, Yeoksam-dong, Gangnam-gu, Soul 135-080
 Toll free: (080) 801-0191   Email: infokorea@gfa.org.kr

NEW ZEALAND PO Box 302580, North Harbour, North Shore City 0751
 Toll free: 0508-918-918   Email: infonz@gfa.org

SOUTH AFRICA P.O. Box 28880, Sunridge Park, Port Elizabeth 6008
 Phone: 041 360-0198   Email: infoza@gfa.org

UNITED KINGDOM PO Box 166, Winterscale House, YORK YO10 5WA
 Phone: 01904 643 233   Email: infouk@gfa.org

UNITED STATES 1800 Golden Trail Court, Carrollton, TX 75010
 Toll free: 1-800-WIN-ASIA   Email: info@gfa.org

Travel to the mission field—
for a few hours

Even though you don't live with the millions of people in South Asia or experience their unique cultures and struggles, you can intercede for them!

By joining in **Gospel for Asia's live-streaming prayer meetings**, you can step inside their world through stories, photos and videos. You might even change, too. Here's what other people said about the prayer meetings:

> "I don't think I ever come away with a dry eye from these prayer meetings. It is so encouraging to me to see the Lord working so mightily in so many ways in the world."
> —Sheri

> "It is so good and helpful to hear of the needs and to sense God's Spirit at work. It helps me to pray more earnestly and to be a part of what God is doing in your ministry." —Timothy

> "Praise Jesus! I love having a team to pray with."
> —Mia

Pray with us!
Go to **www.gfa.org/pray** for schedules and to participate in the streamed prayer meetings.

FREE EMAIL UPDATES
Sign up today at **gfa.org/email**

Hear from today's heroes of the mission field.

Have their stories and prayer requests sent straight to your inbox.

- Fuel your prayer life with compelling news and photos from the mission field.
- Stay informed with links to important video and audio clips.
- Learn about the latest opportunities to reach the lost world.

GFA sends updates every week. You may cancel your free subscription at any time. We will not sell or release your email address for any reason.

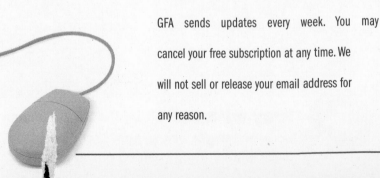